Contents

How to use the CD-ROM

The CD-ROM contains a PDF file, labelled 'Worksheets.pdf', which contains worksheets for each lesson in this resource. You will need Acrobat Reader version 3 or higher to view and print these resources.

The documents are set up to print to A4 but you can enlarge them to A3 by increasing the output percentage at the point of printing using the page set-up settings for your printer.

To photocopy the worksheets directly from this book, set your photocopier to enlarge by 125% and align the edge of the page to be copied against the leading edge of the the copier glass (usually indicated by an arrow).

The Last Unicorn

Is it my responsibility to protect

Exmouth

University of Plymouth Library

Subject to status this item may be renewed
via your Voyager account

http://voyager.plymouth.ac.uk

Exeter tel: (01392) 475049
Exmouth tel: (01395) 255331
Plymouth tel: (01752) 232323

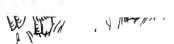

A story and activity based approach

for 8 to 12 year olds

Fiona Angwin and Jeff Foster

Lucky Duck is more than a publishing house and training agency. George Robinson and Barbara Maines founded the company in the 1980s when they worked together as a head and psychologist developing innovative strategies to support challenging students.

They have an international reputation for their work on bullying, self-esteem, emotional literacy and many other subjects of interest to the world of education.

George and Barbara have set up a regular news-spot on the website. Twice yearly these items will be printed as a newsletter. If you would like to go on the mailing list to receive this then please contact us:

Lucky Duck Publishing Ltd, 3 Thorndale Mews, Clifton, Bristol, BS8 2HX, UK

Phone: 0044 (0)117 973 2881 e-mail newsletter@luckyduck.co.uk

Fax: 044 (0)117 973 1707 website www.luckyduck.co.uk

ISBN 1 904 315 10 0

Published by Lucky Duck Publishing Ltd
3 Thorndale Mews, Clifton, Bristol, BS8 2HX, UK

www.luckyduck.co.uk

Commissioning Editor: George Robinson
Editorial Team: Wendy Ogden, Mel Maines, Sarah Lynch
Designer: Helen Weller
Illustrator: Philippa Drakeford

Printed by Antony Rowe Limited

Introduction

The main idea within *The Last Unicorn* is to promote the realisation of what mankind has done, and is still doing, to our world.

It was our intent that the use of a mythical creature would excite the children's imagination and therefore engage them with the story and consequently with the points it aims to make. We also realised that the death of an animal that did not exist in reality would present a parallel with reality for older children to explore whilst not being too confrontational for the younger children.

Time travel and adventures will always appeal to a younger audience and our heroine needs educating as much as any of us. Hopefully, the lessons she learns can be learnt by your pupils without suffering the rigours that Jules endures!

How to use this pack

The course lasts for six lessons and can be followed by the whole class or a smaller group (of ten or more pupils). At the beginning of each lesson there is a chapter of the story. This could be read aloud by the teacher (with pupils following from photocopied sheets) or by the pupils (again using photocopied sheets). Each section of the story will last about 15 minutes, though slower readers may take a little longer to read it aloud.

Following the story, the class or group can use the discussion points to explore some of the ideas the story has just covered. A short activity follows this and leads up to a game which will usually take the remainder of the lesson and will focus on a particular aspect of the chapter they've just read or listened to and its meaning. (Some of the games require one or two simple props, so read ahead and be prepared.)

The aim of the story, discussion points, activities and games is not only to teach the children the lessons that history shows us, and their value for the future, but also the benefit of learning for its own sake.

Jules typifies the Everyman within all of us, who requires the understanding and motivation to take a positive approach to her own environment and to the wider world. We all take our habitat and its occupants, human or not, for granted.

It was Ramshackle Theatre's aim to show that although change is not always easy and does not always happen quickly, the first step to a better future is always the step we take ourselves. Today is where we start to build the future.

The worksheets could be filled in at the end of the lesson, if there is time, or given out as homework to be completed before the next lesson. The worksheets are specifically aimed at individuals, unlike the rest of the material, to ensure that everyone is keeping up with the course, learning from it and applying its lessons to their own behaviour.

At the beginning of the next lesson there is a brief question and answer session to help the pupils remember what has happened in the previous chapters, then the lesson proceeds as above.

Before the lessons there are additional activity suggestions and assembly options. The assembly suggestions are to allow the group or class to share part of what they've learned with the rest of the school.

Background to the pack

The authors, Fiona Angwin and Jeff Foster, worked as Ramshackle Theatre Company for three years, taking plays to primary and younger secondary school pupils across the North West and the Midlands.

The plays usually had a PHSE theme that was explored through the story, was often challenging and always funny. These were regularly followed up with workshops on the same theme, encouraging pupils to think through issues and apply them to their own lives. This means that each piece offered to schools in this series has been tried and tested. The stories appeal to the age groups they're aimed at and the workshop games and activities have all been refined over a number of practical sessions with children of different abilities.

The idea of producing Ramshackle's material as education packs is to enable us to share stories and ideas which we know teachers have found helpful with far more schools than we could visit in person and to make the material available on a more affordable basis.

We hope you enjoy using it!

Stories and Topics presented by Ramshackle Theatre Company

Beauty and The Beast	judging by appearances
Billy's Dreams	bullying and solutions based on empathy
The Blue Bird	the importance of encouragement: getting the best out of people
Bookends	the power of imagination; stories or lies
Down in the Dungeon	facing up to our fears
The Last Unicorn	benefits of learning: shaping the future from lessons of the past
The Magic Box -	progress versus the environment
The Nightingale	real values; reality versus virtuality
Punch and The Pawn	managing anger (available in book form from Lucky Duck)
Saving the Squatlick	appreciating individuality
The Snow Queen	making, breaking and mending friendships
Stoatally Confused	the advantages of co-operation
The Water Babies	treatment of others.

Some of the above also have environmental workshops attached on subjects such as rainforests; predators and prey; endangered species and extinction; trees and forests. This is because the company has a strong commitment to environmental issues and wants to encourage young people to take a positive approach to the world.

National Curriculum Connections

The subject areas in which this material connects to the National Curriculum are Science and History, though there are also PHSE and English connections.

Key Stage 2

Science connections

Living things in their environment

> Pupils learn about:
> ▶ ways in which living things and the environment need protection.

Life processes and living things

> Pupils are encouraged to:
> ▶ apply their knowledge and understanding of scientific ideas to familiar phenomena, everyday things and their personal health
> ▶ think about the positive and negative effects of scientific and technological developments on the environment and in other contexts.

History connections

Chronological understanding

> Pupils learn to:
> ▶ place events, people and changes into correct periods of time
> ▶ use dates and vocabulary relating to the passing of time.

Knowledge and understanding of events, people and changes in the past

> Pupils learn about:
> ▶ characteristic features of the periods and societies studied, including beliefs, ideas, attitudes and experiences of men, women and children in the past
> ▶ the social, cultural, religious and ethnic diversity of the societies studied.

Victorian Britain

> Pupils learn about:
> ▶ the impact of events and changes in work on the lives of men, women and children from different sections of society.

PHSE connections

Developing confidence and responsibility, and making the most of their abilities.

> Pupils are encouraged to:
> ▶ talk and write about their opinions, and explain their views on issues that affect both themselves and society.

Developing good relationships and respecting the differences between people.

> Pupils are encouraged to:
> ▶ think about the lives of people living in other places and times, and people with different values and customs.

Key Stage 3

Science connections

Ideas and evidence in science

Pupils learn about:

▸ the ways in which scientists work today and how they worked in the past..

Pupils are encouraged to:

▸ think about the positive and negative effects of scientific and technological developments on the environment and other contexts taking account of others' views and understand why opinions may differ.

Living things in their environment adaptation and competition

Pupils learn about:

▸ ways in which living things and the environment can be protected, and the importance of sustainable development that habitats support a diversity of plants and animals that are interdependent how predation and competition for resources affect the size of populations.

History connections

Chronological understanding

Pupils learn to:

▸ recognise and make appropriate use of dates, vocabulary and conventions that describe historical periods and the passing of time.

Knowledge and understanding of events, people and changes in the past

Pupils learn:

▸ to describe and analyse the relationships between the characteristic features of the periods and societies studied, including the experiences and range of ideas, beliefs and attitudes of men, women and children in the past

▸ about the social, cultural, religious and ethnic diversity of the societies studied.

Britain 1066-1500

Pupils learn some characteristic features of life.

Britain 1750-1900

Pupils learn about industrialisation and its impact.

English (KS2 & KS3)

This course provides opportunities for speaking and listening. The text can be read aloud by the pupils or the teacher.

The discussion after each section of the story encourages all members of the group or class to contribute their ideas and learn from each other's opinions.

The text encourages discussions on language variation, as different characters, having been originally performed on stage, have contrasting accents and speech patterns.

Extinction and Endangered Species

Extinction

Some animals become extinct through natural causes, such as climate changes. This may account for the extinction of the dinosaurs 65 million years ago – one theory about why they died out is that the world grew too cold for them. Certainly climate changes can have an effect on some animals, even small changes may affect animals which are living at the extreme edges of their natural range.

About 20,000 kinds of plants and animals are facing extinction today. Extinction occurs when beings are competing with wild animals for living space and when animals are killed for enjoyment. We are also destroying the places where rare plants live, collecting too many of them and letting farm animals eat them.

Animals can become extinct within a region, or a country, even if they still exist in other parts of the world. For example, the last mouse-eared bat became extinct in Great Britain in 1994, although there are still a number surviving in other parts of the world, and in Poland a number of measures are being taken to ensure their remaining mouse-eared bats survive.

More commonly, animals and plants may be reduced in number to the point where a species is in danger of total extinction, or becomes extinct entirely due to man-made pressures. These can come in several forms.

Hunting

While man has always hunted animals for food, or for their skins, in order to survive, the escalation of this to a commercial scale and the tendency to over-hunt or over-fish can completely wipe out some target species. For example, there are probably fewer than 4000 tigers left in India. They are now protected by law but poachers still kill them because their claws and bones can be sold to make medicines and their fur still sells for a very high price.

(NB The mythical unicorn was also supposed to have magical healing properties. Had it been a real animal it would undoubtedly have been hunted for its horn and its supposed properties. Rhino have been hunted almost to the point of extinction for exactly this reason.)

The narwhal is a kind of whale that lives in the Arctic seas. The whales are hunted for their spiralled tusk that looks just like a unicorn's horn. If too many narwhals are taken, one day they too may become extinct.

Jaguars are rare because people have hunted them for their fabulous spotted fur. They are also struggling because their rainforest home is being destroyed.

In 1970 there were about 2 million elephants in Africa. Today there are fewer than 500,000 left.

Pollution

When harmful chemicals get into the water, the air or the soil, they cause pollution. This can poison so many animals that the affected species become endangered.

For example, the bald eagle was once close to extinction because the fish on which it depended for food became poisoned by crop spray. The spray had washed off the land into the lakes and poisoned the fish, but once the spray was banned the fish population recovered, as did the bald eagle, which is now thriving.

Destruction of the environment

Some animals are endangered because the places in which they live are cleared to make room for farms, factories, roads or homes, or in the case of forests, because the wood itself is wanted for commercial purposes.

So many animals and plants are endangered for these kinds of reasons that it's hard to pick single examples. The rate at which species are becoming extinct is rising fast, mainly due to the destruction of their habitats.

An example of this is in Indonesia, where the cultivation of durian fruit has given way to the cultivation of rice to feed the growing population. A species of bat used to feed on the durian and now that species is dying. Thousands of species of plant also become extinct when the land is turned over to agriculture, including plants that could have real importance as cures for many of our illnesses. For example, the beautiful rosy periwinkle grows in the rapidly disappearing rainforests on the island of Madagascar. Drugs made from the rosy periwinkle have been used to treat some forms of cancer. When a plant dies out so do all the animals that depend entirely on it for food and shelter. Plants such as the Killarney fern and pitcher-plants are rare because too many of them have been collected from the wild for use in gardens.

Amongst the mammals, a great many species have been driven almost to extinction, such as the golden lion tamarin, which lives in the rainforest. With its habitats rapidly diminishing there are only about 400 of these beautiful primates left in the world.

Direct contact

Even human actions, which are not intentionally harmful, can put some species of animals at risk. For example, the mountain gorillas live in reserves high up in the Virunga Mountains in Africa. People can visit them but the gorillas are not used to common human illnesses. They can die of flu and of measles. To protect the gorillas, visitors have to show they're fit and healthy!

When people move to new parts of the world they often take animals with them. These new animals sometimes hunt the ones that already live there.

For example, the heavy, flightless dodos laid their eggs on the ground which made them easy pickings for the dogs and rats that came to the Island of Mauritius on the ships of explorers and other sailors who stopped off there. The pigs that the settlers introduced on to the island ate the eggs and chicks and helped to drive the birds to extinction.

The pet trade is also responsible for endangering certain species. Spix's macaws have been highly prized as pets. Today there are only 31 left, of which just one lives in the wild. If he doesn't breed with the female that has been released near to him his species will be extinct in the wild. While parrots and other 'attractive' birds and animals have always been a target for the pet trade, even the red-kneed tarantula has been endangered because so many have been taken from the wild to be pets.

Even collectors from museums have been guilty of taking endangered species for their collections – whether national or private. For example, Kitty's hog-nosed bat (otherwise

known as the bumblebee bat because it is only the size of a bumblebee) has the misfortune to be not only the world's smallest bat but also the world's smallest mammal. This meant that every museum collection was keen to have a specimen of it, increasing the pressure on an already endangered species. While many modern museums will now resist this kind of temptation, the professor in the play was typical of his period, being more interested in his specimens as items of his collection rather than animals in their own right.

Conservation

These days conservation is a huge and complicated issue, and often needs planning on a global scale, though most work is done at a national or local level.

Three aspects of conservation need to be tackled to give endangered animals the best chance of survival:

Saving animals

When a species is extremely endangered the first step may be to save individual animals, often by collecting part of the population from the wild and setting them up as a breeding colony in a zoo. This protects the individual animal from the circumstances that were threatening them and allows numbers to build up in safety, in the hope of being able to return them, or their offspring, to the wild. This means many zoos have taken on the role of 'Arks'...not just presenting animals for public spectacle but striving for their survival and using the period of enforced captivity to educate the people that see them. For example, Rodrigues fruit bats live on Rodrigues Island in the Indian Ocean. As a fruit eater it needs a lot of fruit trees to survive, but most of its forest home has been cut down and there were barely 50 left in 1976. Gerald Durrell, the founder of Jersey Zoo, collected 10 at that time (with the consent of the Government of Mauritius) and successful captive breeding increased this to a colony of over a hundred. Some of these have now been spread to other zoos to expand the captive-breeding programme. The long-term aim is to return the offspring to the wild when their habitat has recovered.

One successful example of re-introduction is the world's rarest kestrel, a native of Mauritius, and the Jersey Wildlife Preservation Trust has supported a very successful captive-breeding programme on that island. From a known population of only six individuals in the 1970s, the Mauritius kestrel has steadily grown in numbers and over 200 captive-bred birds have been released into secure sites. It is also reported that several pairs of birds that had been released in earlier years are now breeding successfully in the wild.

Scimitar-horned oryx have probably died out in the wild. Hundreds have been born in zoos though, and some have been sent to live in a national park in Tunisia, North Africa. It is a first step towards re-establishing them in the wild.

Seventy-two years ago, the golden hamster was nearly extinct. Then one female and her 12 young were caught and allowed to breed in safety. Soon there were millions of them, in captivity at least.

Saving habitats

Endangered animals can be returned to the wild if there is a 'wild' left to return them to. This means that protecting habitats must go hand in hand with saving animals, if the animals are to have any hope of a completely natural existence. This can be done by designating areas as 'protected' – turning them into nature reserves and preventing them being exploited for commercial purposes. For example, the Galapagos Islands are the home to plants and animals not found anywhere else in the world. The islands have been turned into a huge national park so that all the wildlife is protected. If protection of an area comes too late, habitats that have been destroyed can sometimes be recreated by careful planting etc.

It can also be useful to leave 'corridors' of vegetation linking one protected habitat to another, so animals can move around safely to find food or mates.

Re-introducing endangered species to the wild can be a complicated business. Often the animals to be returned have grown up, or been bred in captivity and have forgotten, or never learned some of the skills needed to survive in the wild.

For example, when a colony of monkeys was about to be reintroduced in the wild every step was meticulously planned. But when the animals were released into the trees in the area chosen for their new home they kept falling off the branches, despite being very agile in their usual enclosures. Eventually it was realised that the monkeys had problems with real trees because the branches moved when the animals landed on them. The branches in their enclosures looked the same but were fixed at both ends, so the monkeys never learned how to balance on springing branches. The animals had to be collected up and given the chance to learn this new skill before being re-released.

Educating people

As man is the major cause of most animals becoming extinct it is man that needs to learn new ways of relating to wildlife and the environment if this trend towards extinction is to be prevented. This means that educating people is a very important part of conservation.

At a local level this may mean explaining to a native population, which is struggling for its own survival, that they should refrain from hunting creatures that they have always considered 'fair game' or should at least hunt them sparingly, for their own needs and not for sale on a commercial scale, which is difficult if they are dependent on the extra income hunting may bring in.

On a global scale, governments can make laws banning the trade of certain animals or animal products (such as ivory) but these still have to be enforced on a local level.

Even tourists need to be educated so that they don't buy animal products such as skins and shells of endangered creatures as mementos of their trip abroad.

Why bother to conserve endangered species?

Some wild animals provide people with food, clothing and other materials. If the animals disappear, all of these are lost with them. Some animals and many plants are useful medically. For example, the saliva of the vampire bat, which contains an anti-coagulant, is now being used in the treatment of human heart disease. If species die out we may lose something that might be vital for use in the future. The environment is also a delicately balanced organism; if one element is lost from it the remainder must be affected sooner or later.

Besides which, animals make the world a beautiful and interesting place and have a right to exist and to be treated fairly.

But whether the endangered animal is large and appealing, like the giant panda, or small and apparently insignificant like the almost extinct Lord Howe's Island stick insect, the same rules apply. Once an animal is gone, it's gone forever.

Zoos of the future

In the past zoos kept animals just for people to look at and most zoos kept their animals in small groups or even singly, often in cramped conditions. The range of animals was generally predictable with large, 'popular' animals making up the bulk of each collection. So most zoos would have elephants, bears, giraffes, monkeys, apes, parrots, flamingos etc.

Today, many zoos are working hard to breed endangered animals and, hopefully, to return them to the wild. Enclosures are generally larger, Chester Zoo is a good example of a zoo which has always tried to give its animals sufficient space, and the animals are kept in greater numbers to give them more natural social groups and to increase the chances of them breeding successfully. Zoos are tending to specialise more, having fewer types of animals and concentrating on breeding the ones they have in large numbers. A classic example of this is Jersey Zoo founded by Gerald Durrell. This concentrates almost entirely on breeding endangered species and makes no concessions to give 'the public' what they expect to see in a zoo.

As time passes and new animals become endangered, they too may need zoos, as temporary arks, until they can return safely to the wild.

References

Silver, D. & Vallely, B. (1990) *The Young Person's Guide to Saving the Planet*, Virago.

Charman, A. (1996) *I wonder why the Dodo is dead*, Kingfisher.

Taylor, B. (2002) *Going, Going, Gone*, Oxford University Press.

Air Pollution

The air of the planet is being polluted by acid gases, dust, petrol and diesel fumes and poisonous chemicals. These come from cars, factories and power stations.

Acid rain is seen as a major air pollution disaster, but there are other examples. One is the famous brown haze, or smog, which hangs over the Los Angeles basin in California. The chemical compounds in the smog are formed by the sunlight acting on gases in the air that come from vehicles, the burning of fossil fuels and various other industrial processes. They are poisonous, particularly to plants but also to humans. Melbourne, Ankara and Mexico City also suffer from this kind of smog.

Cities in the developing world are beginning to suffer from industries that have been set up near them. Lagos, Jakarta and Calcutta are covered with a build-up of charcoal-caused smoke.

In Victorian times the smoke from the factory chimneys, railways and domestic chimney pots mixed with fog to create what Londoner's called a peasouper, which was a very thick, yellow, heavy-smelling fog. Changes in manufacturing methods and a reduction in the use of coal fires eventually improved the quality of the air. Now governments are having to look at ways to improve the quality of the air we breathe today.

A major problem with air pollution is that it does not obey national boundaries. Wind cycles and currents can carry pollution hundreds of miles away from its original source. So Britain is a large contributor to air pollution in Sweden and creates more for Norway than Norway does itself. The pollutants of the USA end up on the eastern coast of Canada.

Cigarette smoke is also a pollutant, containing a variety of poisonous substances. The poisons in cigarettes include dioxins that are present in the tobacco and in the bleached white cigarette paper. These are released when the cigarettes are burned.

Many countries in the world are trying to solve the problem of air pollution in various ways, either by trying to burn their fossil fuels more cleanly, or by fitting catalytic converters to their cars so that fewer poisonous gases are produced.

Reference

Silver, D. & Vallely, B. (1990) *The Young Person's Guide to Saving the Planet*, Virago.

Asthma

The word 'asthma' is used as a blanket term to cover a condition characterised by episodes of breathlessness caused by intermittent narrowing of the bronchial tubes (or airways) within the lung.

There are many factors that contribute to the development of asthma in the first instance and many that can induce attacks. These will vary from individual to individual.

The best definition is that asthma is a condition in which the airways within the lung are inflamed and so are more sensitive to specific factors (triggers) that cause the airways to narrow, reducing air flow through them and making the individual breathless and/or wheezy.

So asthma is not one disease; it covers a multitude of different patterns. Under that general heading you will find a range of severity, a range of triggering factors and a range of outcomes. It logically follows that what is good for one asthmatic person may be unsuitable for another.

Asthma is a very individual condition and management needs to be personalised because of the variety of factors that underlie each individual's asthma.

Trigger Factors

- exercise
- allergens
- fumes, dust and odours
- colds and viruses
- emotions and stress
- climate and pollution
- cold air, foods and occupational triggers.

Inhalers

Relievers

Bronchodilator drugs are given in inhaled form and act by relaxing the muscle in the walls of the airways, allowing the airway to open up and the air to get in and out more easily. The result is that breathing is eased.

Preventers

These drugs act by reducing the inflammation in the airways, thus calming their irritability. In contrast to reliever inhalers they must be taken on a regular basis, usually twice a day.

Reference

Ayres, J. Prof. (1997) *Understanding Asthma - Family Doctor Series*, Family Doctor Publications.

Unicorns

The unicorn is a mythical and heraldic animal, represented by mediaeval writers as having the legs of a buck, the tail of a lion, the head and body of a horse and a single horn, white at the base, black in the middle and red at the top, in the middle of its forehead. The mediaeval notions concerning it are summarised in the following extract:

"The unicorn has but one horn in the middle of its forehead. It is the only animal that ventures to attack the elephant; and so sharp is the nail of its foot that with one blow it can rip the belly of that beast. Hunters can catch the unicorn only by placing a young virgin in his haunts. No sooner does he see the damsel, than he runs towards her, and lies down at her feet, and so suffers himself to be captured by the hunters. The unicorn represents Jesus Christ, who took upon Him our nature in the virgin's womb, was betrayed by the Jews and delivered into the hands of Pontius Pilate. Its one horn signifies the Gospel of Truth."

Le Bestiaire Divin de Guillaume, Clere de Normandie (13th Century)

Another popular belief was that the unicorn, by dipping its horn into a liquid, could detect whether or not it contained poison. The unicorn is one of the most ancient of mythological beasts for its history can be traced back to the earliest written traditions of ancient Mesopotamia.

It is likely that the unicorn found its way into European mythology via the crusaders returning from the Holy Wars in Syria and Palestine. It became a popular addition to the Bestiaries of the Middle East.

In mythology, man has often persecuted the unicorn, mainly for the magical and medicinal qualities of its horn. If powdered unicorn horn is drunk, the recipient will not suffer from spasms, epilepsy or be poisoned. The horn represents the power of the beast and physicians used to supply rhinoceros horn, representing it to be the horn of a unicorn, to be used as a medicine. Oryx or Narwhal horns were used to counterfeit the horn of the unicorn, which was also considered to be an aphrodisiac.

Belief in the unicorn stretches back into the mists of time, but the most amazing stories were written about him in the romance tales of the Middle Ages. At that time European people believed just as strongly in the unicorn as they did in the elephant and the panther, two other mysterious animals that they had been told about but never had the opportunity to see.

Chinese fables of the unicorn said that, although it lived alone on the edge of the world, it would materialise like a fairy godmother when the king of the country was in trouble.

There are even references to the unicorn in the Bible, all in the Old Testament. They are always referred to as if they were actual, rather than fantasy, animals and are characterised as having strength, ferocity, wildness and unconquerable spirit. However, no one has been able to identify with any certainty which real animal they had confused the unicorn with, or why it became involved in the Christian symbolism of the Middle Ages.

The unicorn is also one of the most popular of the heraldic beasts and is seen in the Royal Arms of England where it appears with the lion. There was supposed to be great rivalry between the unicorn and the lion for the title of King of Beasts – hence the nursery rhyme:

> The lion and the unicorn
> Were fighting for the crown
> The lion chased the unicorn
> All around the town.

Symbolically the fight between a real beast and a fabulous one represented the conflict between realistic and fanciful tendencies.

The last story from the heraldic imagery is how the unicorn, chasing the lion, buries its horn in a tree and is completely stuck. The lion leaps on it and kills it.

References

Hargreaves, J. (1990) *Hargreaves New Illustrated Bestiary*, Gothic Image Publication.

Miller, C. (1974) *A Dictionary of Monsters and Mysterious Beasts*, Piccolo.

Shepard, O. (1930) *The Lore of the Unicorn*, Senate.

Brewer's Dictionary of Phase & Fable (1975), Cassell & Company Ltd.

World Bible Publishing, *The Holy Bible: King James Version*, (1989), Bible Publishers Inc. (No. 23:22, No. 24:8, Job 39:9, Job 39:10, Psalm 92:10, Psalm 20:6, Psalm 22:21, Deut.33:17, Isiah 34:7)

Historical Periods

The mediaeval period

The mediaeval period visited in the story was in the time in which King John ruled, over the years 1199-1216.

King John

When he came to the throne he held lands in Anjou and Normandy, but early in his reign he lost these in battle to King Philip of France.

John spent the next ten years taxing his subjects, especially the richer ones, very heavily to pay for a great military alliance against France to try and win the lands back.

However, the allied army was defeated in 1214 at the Battle of Bouvines. By now the English had had enough of paying high taxes and being led by the barons, they rebelled.

The citizens of London opened their gates to the rebels, which forced John to meet their leaders at Runnymeade by the River Thames in 1215. There he was forced to make promises, which were written down in the treaty, which later became known as the Magna Carta.

King John promised to treat everyone more fairly and agreed to have a committee of twenty-five barons to whom people could complain if they thought the king was failing to keep his promises.

However, John did not keep his promises and many of the barons then chose Louis, the son of Philip of France, to be King of England, and in May 1216, a French army held London and Winchester. When King John died in 1216 the country he ruled over was divided by civil war. As a king he had been a failure, losing Normandy, Anjou and much of England too.

John's eldest son, Henry, was only nine at the time, so a number of barons formed a council to defeat Louis and govern until Henry III was old enough to rule for himself. The French were beaten in battle and the council re-issued the Magna Carta to show that they intended to govern the country better than King John had done. From now on the Magna Carta (the big charter) became a symbol of good government.

Farming

At this time most people lived and worked on small farms. They kept livestock such as cattle, sheep, pigs and poultry, which gave them meat, milk, eggs, leather and woollen clothing. They kept bees for honey and horses and oxen for pulling carts and ploughs. Food that they were able to preserve and keep, such as bacon, sausages and cheese, was especially useful. The crops they grew were mainly grain, used for making bread and ale.

The lives of mediaeval peasants were inextricably linked to the natural cycle, to the weather and to the rhythm of the seasons. They went to bed when the light faded and rose early with the sun. Most families rented a small strip of land in the large, open fields, paying a percentage of the yield to the lord or church as a tithe. Most of the work was done by hand.

Livestock was fenced in using wattle hurdles, made from hazel. Uprights were driven into the ground and interwoven with a mixture of rounded-driven strips of wood.

Much of the wealth of the Middle Ages was founded on the wool trade. Most families took part in sheep shearing in June, using handshears.

Corn was threshed after harvesting. Beating the straw using jointed wooden flails separated the grain.

Most fabrics were made from wool and linen. Spinning and weaving were domestic chores usually undertaken by women in the house. Children helped with carding – untangling the raw fabric.

In the country both boys and girls were expected to help their parents with the farm work – weeding, stone-picking, drawing and fetching water from the well, helping with the animals, gathering berries and picking fruit.

As they grew older, boys and girls began to go separate ways. Brothers and sisters stopped sharing the same bed. Boys joined in their fathers' work: ploughing, reaping, building or staying out in the fields with sheep and cattle. Girls stayed with their mothers: cooking, baking, cleaning, spinning and weaving. By the time they were fourteen both boys and girls had been trained for their future roles in life.

Hunting

For the poor, supplementing the diet by hunting wild animals on common land was essential, but if they were caught poaching on the lord's estate they would be severely punished and persistent offenders might be executed.

From Norman times nearly one quarter of England came under 'forest law'. Forests were vast tracts of land used by the king and his nobles as hunting preserves. The land did not always have tree cover, but as much of it did the word 'forest' has come to be associated with dense woodland.

For youths from wealthy families, fowling provided good archery practice. The dog was used to fetch any birds shot and brought to the ground. When proficient, the youths progressed to hawking or hunting with their fathers. Hawking and hunting with dogs were popular pursuits for the rich. They became great social events and even ladies took part in the sport.

The Victorian period

The year visited in this period was 1840, not long after Queen Victoria came to the throne.

Queen Victoria

Queen Victoria was born in 1819. She ascended to the throne in 1837 and ruled until she died in 1901.

The previous king, William IV, had made himself unpopular by meddling in political affairs. The king before him, George IV, had been a rotten husband, glutton and a drunk.

By contrast, Victoria was perfect. She didn't interfere too much in politics, nor did she behave badly. Instead, she and her husband, Albert, worked hard, lived simply and spent much of their spare time with their nine children.

After the scandalous goings-on of previous monarchs, Victoria and Albert's devotion to each other was a welcome change and their example of family life was one that many Victorians tried to follow. Victoria and Albert made the royal family popular. Their mixture of ordinariness and wealth made it easy for prosperous Victorians to identify with them and respect them.

The Industrial Revolution

The term generally denotes the whole range of technological and economic changes, which transformed Great Britain from an essentially rural society into an urban industrialised state. The dates usually assigned to this period of change vary somewhat, but are generally thought to run from 1750 to 1850, so the year visited in the story is towards the end of this period, when the changes had started to affect the whole country.

Britain's growth as a great industrial and manufacturing nation was largely due to the improvement of the steam engine in the 1780s. Before steam engines had been invented only wind, water, people or horses could power machines. Machines driven by steam were not only more reliable, they were quicker too. Smart businessmen soon realised that by using steam powered machinery they could produce goods more cheaply than ever before. So they built factories to house the monstrous new machines and employed lots of people to work in them.

Some Victorian farmers bought steam powered machines to help them produce the extra food needed to feed Britain's growing population. These machines meant that fewer workers were needed, so many farm hands moved to the cities and towns that were springing up around factories to find work. Rows of poor quality terraced slums sprang up around the factories to house them.

Life in the country

Many people's houses were tied to their jobs, so if they lost their employment they lost their homes too. This made the move to the cities to work in the factories even more necessary.

As the population moved to the towns many villages lost their weekly market as more and more of the food produced was taken to the towns to sell. A single village shop, selling a range of goods, could usually satisfy the needs of most rural communities.

Although generally less well-off than town dwellers, those who lived in the country usually had a better quality of life and could expect to live longer – to about 50 years of age compared to 40 for those in the town. Although many of those who worked in the country still lived in primitive one-roomed cottages, living conditions and sanitation were much better than in towns.   .

Life in towns

During the 1800s many workers lived in rows of 'back-to-back' houses which were built close to the factories where they worked. Dreary, damp and overcrowded, these houses had neither piped water nor indoor toilets. Families had to collect their water from street taps or rivers, and share outdoor toilets with their neighbours. These toilets were often no more than a shed with a seat built over a pit in the ground. The smelly waste that collected in the pits was removed after dark by the 'night soil men' and sold to farmers as fertiliser.

As there were no proper sewers, dirty water and human waste were often left to drain away in the streets. When this mulch, along with factory waste, seeped into the water supplies, those that drank the water often caught dreadful diseases like cholera and typhoid.

Workers' houses were very overcrowded. Sometimes an entire family had to live in one room, which meant diseases could spread quickly.

Poverty was so bad in most towns that many people resorted to crime in the dingy streets. The old and infirm, particularly, often fell victim to pickpockets. Many children, deprived of sunlight and clean air and fed a poor, unbalanced diet, developed rickets, a debilitating disease causing bone malformation. Fresh milk containing plenty of Vitamin D helped to reduce the incidence of the disease.

To keep costs low, factory owners often paid unskilled workers very poor wages. This meant that whole families, including children, had to work long hours just to earn enough money to eat. Looking after factory machinery was an unskilled job, so many employers preferred to use women and children because they could be paid lower wages. Very young children were useful in cloth-making factories because they were small enough to crawl under machines that were still running. The moving parts of the machinery were rarely covered so horrific accidents were common. The long hours spent in dark, dusty, noisy factories meant that many children grew up weak and sickly.

Those not working in factories could try to make a living on the streets. Traders sold their wares, such as bread, milk and pies, from handcarts. Girls might sell cut flowers while boys might offer fresh poultry or a shoeshine.

It was not uncommon for couples to have as many as nine or ten children and the whole family was expected to work. Children could be sent out to work as young as five years old, but even those not sent to the factories had to do chores around the house or help make items to sell. In early Victorian times many children did not go to school. A variety of schools were provided for them but since schooling was not compulsory, and rarely free, many poor children did not attend.

It was also thought that educating working class children would make them discontented with their lot. The fortunate few went to dame schools, charitable institutions run by women in their own homes, where reading, writing and simple arithmetic were taught.

Homelessness was a constant problem in towns, especially for those who were unable to work and were put out on to the streets. Alcohol was cheap and easier to acquire than good drinking water, so drunkenness was a problem, even amongst children.

For many poor city families, meals consisted mainly of bread, potatoes, cheese, tea and porridge, with perhaps a bit of bacon when they could afford it. While in the past most people had worked on the land and produced most of their own food, now they worked in factories, had no land or gardens and had to buy all their food out of their wages. This marked the beginning of the modern consumer society.

This left people at the mercy of corrupt shopkeepers, who watered down their milk and added plaster to their flour and sulphuric acid to their vinegar.

Homeless families with nowhere to go except the parish workhouse probably had the worst diet of all. In return for work, such as breaking stones and crushing bones for glue, they were given a roof over their heads and cheap food, such as gruel. Gruel is a soup-like porridge made by boiling oatmeal in water or milk. Served with a slice of coarse bread, it is watery and unpleasant, and formed the staple diet of workhouse inmates.

References

Gillingham, J. (2001) *Medieval Kingdoms of Alfred the Great*, Henry VII, The Young Oxford History of Britain & Ireland, Oxford University Press.

Guy, J. (1995) *Medieval Life, Snapping-turtle guide*, Addax Retail Publishing Ltd in association with Bodleian Library.

Guy, J. (1997) *Victorian Life, Snapping-turtle guide*, Ticktock Publishing Ltd U.K.

Wright, R (1994) *The Victorians*, Franklin Watts.

Additional Activities (Optional)

Essay titles or extended discussion points:

A.   If you could travel through time, where would you go and why?

B.   If you could change one thing that people have done to the environment, in the

past or the present, what would it be and why?

Encourage the pupils to try and discover what, if anything, was on the site of their school in the past (before the school was built).

Encourage the pupils to draw a map of the area and mark different types of habitat on it, e.g. meadow, urban green space, woodland etc.

As a group, come up with a plan for protecting a habitat or habitats near the school (or in the grounds). Include practical ideas that the pupils can get involved in, like litter picking, building and putting up bird and bat boxes, creating a pond etc.

Have a group discussion about the practical ways in which people can help protect the environment on a global level, e.g. using renewable resources, saving energy, recycling, reducing consumption, learning to repair and reuse things instead of disposing of them.

Assembly suggestions

The text in this play doesn't lend itself to short, scripted performances in assemblies, as many of the ideas are developed throughout the play, rather than in concise moments.

However, it would be possible to share the theme the children have been following by sharing one of the games, and its meaning, with the whole school.

The most appropriate game for this would be 'Threes' because it can be played in a crowded school hall, and doesn't require 'running around' space, but 'Greedy Monkeys' could also be used.

Answer Sheet

For factual questions on worksheets.

Worksheet 1 Island Challenge

There are no correct answers to these questions. The idea is to get the children thinking. If they alter any of their colonisation plans in their final answer, they have been willing to learn from history.

Worksheet 2 Companionship

Animals that live alone (other than when breeding):

   tigers, jaguars, mountain lions (pumas), polar bears, moles.

Animals that live in groups:

   rabbits, bats, elephants, badgers, zebras, chimpanzees, wolves.

Worksheet 3 Need versus Greed

Again there are no correct answers; the questions are just to encourage the children to think.

Worksheet 4 Habitats

Missing words:

   plants

   cows

   microbes

   soil

   birds

   bats

   water.

Worksheet 5 Building a Zoo

Again, a game designed to get children to think about the issues, rather than come up with correct answers.

Worksheet 6 Co-operation

This sheet, too, is about exploring ideas, not coming up with the right answer.

Lesson 1

Jules takes a test and sets off on a journey

There was a hushed silence in the school hall as the pupils leaned forward to hear the announcement.

Miss Denton, deputy head of St Peter's Primary School, walked to the middle of the stage and smiled. She wore a flowery summer dress and shiny, light blue shoes. It was the shoes that made you think that there was more to Miss Denton than met the eye. All the other teachers wore sensible shoes in brown or black, the sort of shoes you didn't even notice. Miss Denton's shoes sparkled, as did her eyes when she smiled. Miss Denton smiled most of the time. In fact, the only times she stopped smiling were when a pupil let her down and most of the pupils didn't want to do that.

"This morning," said Miss Denton, "we have arranged a little treat for you. You've been working so hard this term that the staff felt you all deserved it – well, most of you, anyway."

Miss Denton's eyes scanned the assembled pupils and fixed on Juliette Baylis. Juliette didn't deserve a treat and Miss Denton knew it. So did Juliette, or Jules, as her friends called her. Mind you, Jules didn't have that many friends, she was a bit of a loner. She was the bane of Miss Denton's life, but to be fair Miss Denton was also the bane of hers.

Usually Jules was the one pupil who could wipe the smile off Miss Denton's face. This morning the deputy head just smiled more broadly than ever when she caught sight of her most difficult pupil. Jules squirmed uncomfortably and started fidgeting with her plaits. She had long, reddish blonde hair, which never looked tidy. It was only nine o'clock in the morning, and already strands of it had escaped from the plaits, and were curling round her face and getting in her eyes. These were green and, like her hair, clashed horribly with her maroon school uniform, which was just one of the reasons she hated wearing it.

"We've got a special guest in school this morning," Miss Denton continued, "who has come here to entertain you. I'd like you all to make him very welcome. His name is Marvello the Magnificent and he is a magician!"

There was polite applause from most of the pupils and a few groans from the Year Sixes, who thought they were too old for this kind of entertainment.

Then there was a puzzled silence, because the pupils couldn't see anybody on stage apart from Miss Denton and she was moving to the side, back to her seat. The children started to whisper to each other, wondering what was going on. Suddenly, there was a great flash of light on stage. A cloud of smoke appeared and out of it stepped the strangest looking person any of the children had ever seen.

He wore a long flowing robe which reached right down to his feet and seemed to change colour as you looked at it. One minute it seemed brown, the next it was green, or gold, or copper-coloured. For one horrible moment Jules thought it looked maroon, her least favourite colour. Then she blinked and it was russet instead. The colours seemed to swirl across the robe like clouds across the sky. The effect was almost hypnotic, making it hard to tear your eyes away from the robe to look at the man.

He was tall and thin and had a very wrinkled sort of face. It was hard to tell if the wrinkles were due to old age, or if they were laughter lines. His eyes were blue, or grey or both, and every child in the audience thought he was looking straight at them. His voice, when he spoke, sounded soft, like velvet. He didn't seem to be speaking loudly at all, but everyone in the room could hear him quite clearly, even the Year Sixes lounging against the back wall. Not that they were lounging now. As soon as the magician had appeared they leaned forward to watch him, as fascinated as the rest of the pupils.

"I hate to contradict Miss Denton," said the man, "but I'm not precisely a magician, I'm more of a wizard. However, I am delighted to be invited into your school like this. Of course, it is a little different to the school I went to. There are so many of you, for a start. There were just a handful of us. Two or three hopeful young people desperately trying to learn how to cast spells, how to master the elements of time and space...in short, how to become wizards, philosophers, magicians, call us what you will. Of course, it was all a very long time ago, but I can still remember the lessons. I spent hours practising magic, trying to change one thing into another." He looked at the pupils and grinned. "I still enjoy changing things."

The pupils wriggled nervously, each of them convinced for a moment that they were about to be changed into something. Instead, the wizard, or whatever he was, threw a pile of feathers up into the air and from the middle of this fluttering swirl a dove appeared and flew upwards, circling the hall, until it spotted an open window and flew out through it. The pupils breathed a sigh of relief. He was just an ordinary magician after all. They settled back to enjoy the show.

An hour later the performance was over and the children were filing out into the playground for an early break. The little ones, of course, were convinced the man really was a wizard and that they had been watching pure magic. The older children, however, were debating how he had created the illusions.

"It's all done with mirrors," said one of the Year Sixes. "My dad says all magicians work like that."

"No it's not," argued a Year Five girl, "I think he hypnotised us into seeing what he wanted us to see."

"What does it matter?" Jules asked, joining the queue to leave the hall. "It's over now." Just then Miss Denton caught Jules' eye and called her back. Jules trudged sulkily up the steps leading on to the stage. Now what had she done?

"Juliette," said Miss Denton. "I'd like you to meet Marvello the Magnificent."

"Why?" asked Jules sullenly.

"Because he wants to meet you," Miss Denton said firmly and turned to the man. "Here's the child I was telling you about."

"Delighted to meet you, Jules," said the magician.

"Juliette! Only my friends call me Jules," snapped Jules.

"Oh, I see, fussy about names, are you? Then I'd better tell you mine", said the man.

"I know yours," said Jules. "Marvello the Magnificent."

"That's just my stage name," said the man. "My real name is Malkezawiz."

"Malkez..a..what?"asked Jules puzzled. "I can't even say it."

"Of course, I do have a shorter name, but since you insist on me calling you Juliette, I insist on your calling me Malkezawiz."

"I don't need to call you anything," said Jules stubbornly. "I don't need to talk to you at all."

"I'm afraid that's where you're wrong," said the man. "You see, we need you to settle an argument between Miss Denton and myself. We were talking about school and lessons and so on, and I said even the most empty-headed pupil these days knows a lot more than children did in the past and Miss Denton said that I hadn't met you."

As the insult sank in, Jules glared at Miss Denton, who just smiled back at her, which was really irritating.

"So we wondered," he continued, "if you'd settle the matter for us once and for all. It would mean taking a small test."

"Really, Malkezawiz," said Miss Denton firmly. "I don't think Juliette is up to it. She hates tests, always come bottom of the class."

"Is she really so stupid?" the man asked. Jules frowned as they talked about her as if she wasn't there.

"Oh no," said Miss Denton. "She's not stupid at all, she's just...uncooperative."

"In that case," said the magician, "she wouldn't be willing to take part in a test at all, even if it was going to prove you wrong."

"Yes, I would," interrupted Jules, determined to wipe the smile off Miss Denton's face. "I don't mind taking your test."

"But you don't know enough dear," Miss Denton stated.

"That's not true," Jules was indignant. "I know about lots of things."

"Like what?" asked the man.

"Well, I know about the environment," said Jules. "I'm good at animals and all that stuff."

"Then it would be much too easy to test you on that," the man replied. "Besides, you don't know as much about "the environment" as you think you do. No ... I'll test you on ... History."

"History?" shrieked Jules, horrified. "What's that got to do with anything? It's just a waste of time." History was Jules' least favourite subject. It was also the subject Miss Denton loved most.

"First question," the man continued, "what happened in 1066?"

Jules hesitated. The date did sound familiar. She made a wild guess at it. "The Great Fire of London."

"No," said the man, "that was 1666."

"The Plague, then."

"No, that was 1665. If we're going to work backwards through history, one year at a time, this could take forever."

"I give up then," said Jules crossly. "What did happen in...whenever it was?"

"The Battle of Hastings, of course," Miss Denton said smugly.

"We'll try again, shall we?" asked the magician. "Why was Hadrian's wall built?"

"To keep the Hadrians out?" suggested Jules desperately.

"Don't be ridiculous," said the man. "One more question. Who discovered America?"

"Easy," said Jules, relieved. "Christopher Columbus."

"Wrong," replied the man triumphantly. Jules looked confused. So, for that matter, did Miss Denton.

"You're looking at things the wrong way," the man continued. "The Native Americans lived there long before Columbus landed, so how could he have discovered it?"

"Then that's a stupid question," said a frustrated Jules.

"Now you're thinking," the magician said. "It's all very well knowing the right answer to a question, but it's much more important to know which question to ask."

"Well, I don't care about the questions or the answers," said Jules, "especially if the subject's history. Who needs it?"

"We all do," he replied. "Without understanding what caused things to happen in the past, how can we stop them from happening again in the future?"

"What kind of things?" asked Jules.

"Things like the destruction of the environment. If people refuse to learn from the past they'll just keep making the same mistakes over and over again. That's why you're about to have a crash course."

"In what?" asked Jules, nervously.

"History… the environment… who knows? I can only present you with a situation. What you learn from it is up to you."

"I don't want to learn," said Jules.

"We've noticed," said Miss Denton sharply.

"Besides, it's too late to argue," said the magician. "You've already agreed to take the test."

"I've done the test," said Jules surprised. "All that 1066 stuff."

"That test was just to show you things you didn't know. This test is to teach you why you need to know them." Seeing Jules' bewildered expression he explained. "Look, I'll give you an example. You know you need to keep your inhaler with you all the time, don't you?"

"Yes, of course, I do," said Jules, feeling the reassuring bump of it in her pocket.

"But why do you need it? That's the important question."

"Because it helps me to breathe when there's smoke or fumes in the air, and I have an asthma attack."

"Exactly," said the man. "So you remember to carry your inhaler, not just because you've been told to, but because you know for yourself how important it is, don't you, Juliette? Juliette?"

Jules was staring at him in amazement. How did he know she used an inhaler? Had Miss Denton told him? Did Miss Denton even know? Jules had never used the inhaler in her lessons. Could the man really be...well, magic? Not that Jules believed in such stuff and the tricks he'd done for the school, well, they were just tricks, weren't they? But there was something unusual about him. Jules realised that close up she seemed to be able to see pictures forming in the colours moving across his robe. They disappeared even as she focused on them, but she was sure they were there.

When the robe was green it seemed to be made up of a pattern of leaves, but as it turned to grey it was more like a surface covered in rounded pebbles or cobbles. Then streaks of yellow appeared in it, shifting to look like withered grass. Then the robe was green again, with something pale moving swiftly amongst the leaves, but Jules couldn't quite work out what it was.

"Juliette!" repeated the man, magician, wizard...whatever he was. Jules tore her eyes away from his robe and looked at his face. "Are you alright?" he asked, concerned. Jules nodded, uncertain what to say next. This was unusual for her, because she generally had a clever answer to everything.

"Ready for the test now?" he asked, and handed her a carved wooden box. It looked very old and the carvings on it were of leaves and birds and animals, but they were worn almost smooth from being handled over the years. "Use it carefully," he added, then he turned to Miss Denton. Jules thought she saw him wink at the teacher and Miss Denton wink back, but she decided she must have imagined it. The two adults walked down the steps of the stage and out of the hall, heading for the staff room. She heard Miss Denton offer the magician a cup of coffee before he left and he accepted gratefully. Then Jules was alone on the stage, with the box in her hands.

"I wonder what's in it?" she thought. "I didn't see him use it on stage." She opened the lid and looked inside. It seemed to be full of mist, shifting and changing, like the patterns on the magician's robe. The mist twisted itself into the shape of leaves and branches and started to rise out of the box. Jules slammed the lid down fast. Whatever the stuff was she didn't want it to escape.

She looked up from the box and gasped. In the two or three seconds she'd been looking into the box, everything around her had changed. The stage had disappeared and the hall and the school itself! All that was left was Jules and the box she was holding. Everything else was gone and in its place was a dense, dark forest. Jules screamed.

Discussion points:

1. Why did Miss Denton choose Jules?

2. Is history important?

Activity

Ask the pupils to imagine that they had to go somewhere they'd never been before. The place that they're travelling to is some distance away. Do they think they'd be able to go straight to it, or might they make mistakes along the way and get lost?

What if somebody had already made the journey and written down the route? Would that make it easier? If there was a map of the journey, would that help? Most pupils will think that it would.

What would they think of someone who was given a map of the journey but didn't bother to look at it, because they wanted to make their own mistakes? They will probably think that person is being foolish.

Point out that history can be a bit like a map. It teaches you what people did the first time they were in a particular situation and shows you the mistakes they made, as well as the things that they got right. If you learn from history, it helps you not to make the same mistakes that were made in the past. If you don't bother to learn from it, it's a bit like throwing away the map for your journey and insisting on starting from scratch each time. This means you are likely to make the same mistakes over and over again.

Freeze Frame Game

Split the class up into small groups (6 pupils per group – you need even numbers of pupils per group if possible). Give each group a number. Explain that you are going to ask each group to create a frozen moment in time, based on a well-known incident in history. They have to create that moment using their bodies like statues. Each group must use all of its members in the freeze frame and the pupils can represent objects and buildings as well as people. The rest of the class will have to guess what the moment is and try to remember the image created.

Give out the historical moments, one to each group. You can just tell them, or you can write it on slips of paper for them if you think that will help.

Suggestions for these moments are:

The Battle of Hastings	1066
King John signing the Magna Carta	1215
The Plague	1665
The Great Fire of London	1666
The Coronation of Queen Victoria	1837
The first moon landing (Neil Armstrong & Buzz Aldrin)	1969

These are just our suggestions; feel free to use any moment in history you think the pupils will be familiar with.

If a group doesn't know anything at all about their moment in history give them another suggestion to work on.

Let the groups have 2-3 minutes to decide how to create their moment.

Then get each group to show their freeze frame to the rest of the class, who must guess the moment and try to memorise the positions.

When all the groups have shown their images, tell them that they are now going to recreate another group's image, e.g. Group 1 will present Group 2's image, Group 2 present Group 3's and so on..

They have only one minute to work out how to recreate the image, as well as they can remember it, and they can't ask the other groups for help.

Now get each group to show the image they have tried to copy. The original group can say if it's like theirs or not. The winning group is the one who most closely copies the image they've been asked to reproduce.

They've won because they've concentrated and learnt the moment in history they were presented with. (This team could be rewarded with a sweet each if you choose to use a reward system. If you're going to do this, tell them when you explain the game to give them an incentive.)

Ask the children if they thought replicating the other group's image was an easy or hard exercise. They will probably say quite hard, which you can use to demonstrate to them how easily something can be forgotten, even if it is in the very recent past.

Finish by telling them that this was only a game and it didn't really matter if they didn't learn anything from history well enough to get the image right. Point out that there are real situations in which it would matter a lot. For example, in the situation presented to them on the Island Challenge Worksheet.

Give out Island Challenge A. When the class have completed the sheet, give out part B and discuss the implications.

The Last Unicorn: Lesson 1 Worksheet

Island Challenge A

Imagine you have landed on an uninhabited tropical island. There are about a hundred of you and you decide as a group to settle there. It is the seventeenth century, so living conditions will be fairly basic, and you arrived by ship so your only supplies are things that might be aboard.

The island has no native mammals except bats. There are various pigeons and parakeets up in the trees and a large, flightless pigeon that lives on the ground. There are herds of Giant tortoises and a few other reptiles. There is plenty of clean water in the rivers and streams. On your ship you have some pigs, a couple of dogs and, of course, there are some ship's rats.

Read each question below then tick the box that best describes what you think you would do. (In some cases you may tick more than one box.)

Would you try to build houses?	☐	Yes
	☐	No
If you decide to build, what material would you use?	☐	Timber from ship
	☐	Trees from the island
How would you feed yourselves?	☐	Hunting
	☐	Fishing
	☐	Farming
	☐	All three
If you decide to farm, what spaces will you use?	☐	Plant in the space between the trees
	☐	Cut down trees to make spaces big enough to farm
What animals will you bring ashore from the ship?	☐	Pigs
	☐	Dogs
	☐	Rats
What animals will you hunt for food?	☐	Bats
	☐	Ground dwelling pigeons
	☐	Parakeets
	☐	Giant tortoises
	☐	Fish

The Last Unicorn: Lesson 1 Worksheet

Island Challenge B

The situation described above is exactly what happened on the Island of Mauritius. Sailors first landed there in 1598 and Dutch colonists settled on the island in 1638. By the 1680s the large flightless pigeons (the famous dodo) was extinct. Despite the fact that it didn't taste very nice and so wasn't often hunted for food, the dodo died out very rapidly.

This was mainly due to the animals the settlers introduced. While dogs would have hunted some of the dodos and the rats attacked their eggs and chicks, the main culprits were the pigs. These competed with the dodos for food, disrupted their courtship rituals and their nests, ate their eggs and chicks and drove them towards extinction. At the same time the dodos would have been losing habitat as the humans took over the island.

The Giant tortoises were also hunted to extinction and used for food ashore and on board ships.

Now you know this information, is there anything you would do differently in your plan to colonise the island? Write down these changes below:

_____
_____
_____
_____
_____
_____
_____
_____
_____
_____
_____
_____
_____
_____
_____
_____
_____

If you altered any of your plans, you've been willing to learn from history and not repeat the mistakes of the past.

Lesson 2

Jules meets a fabulous beast and makes a big decision

Recap

Question: Who was the mysterious stranger who came to the school?

Answer: A wizard who came to perform a magic show.

Question: Why did Miss Denton choose Jules to take the test?

Answer: Because Jules needed to learn to learn.

Question: What subject did the wizard particularly want Jules to think about?

Answer: History.

Jules' scream echoed through the woods. The quiet that followed it was unnerving. It was as if the forest itself had frozen. For a few seconds all was silent but then gradually, the forest returned to normal. Birds started to sing and small creatures rustled in the grass beside her feet. Jules stared slowly round trying to take in what had happened. One minute she'd been in school, the next she was in the middle of a forest. How? All she'd done was open the box the magician had given her. No, he wasn't just a magician. No ordinary magician could do this – transport somebody to a completely different place in seconds.

"He really is a wizard," Jules said to herself, amazed. "And he's sent me here on purpose, but why? How am I supposed to get home?" At this thought, Jules began to panic. How was she supposed to get home when she didn't even know where she was?

Trying to keep her fear under control she started to take a look at the forest around her. It was much thicker than any forest she'd seen before. The trees were close together and cast deep shadows. A few feet away there was a clearing, which was bathed in sunlight and flowers of different colours were growing there. Jules moved nervously towards the clearing, wanting to get out of the shadows, which she was beginning to find creepy. Across the clearing a squirrel scampered up a tree trunk.

"That's funny," thought Jules, "it doesn't look like the squirrels in the local park."

The squirrel jumped to another tree and she caught a glimpse of its fur in the sunlight.

"Of course, it's a red squirrel, that's why it looks different...but there are hardly any of those left and none near us. I must be in a completely different part of the country."

She sank down on to the grass in despair. "How am I going to get home?" Even the flowers she was squashing looked unfamiliar. She reached for her inhaler, wanting to be sure it was still safely in her pocket. It was, not that she'd need it here. The air seemed to be really clean. All she could smell were the scents of the forest, no cars or smoke or fumes. Still, it was a relief to know she had her inhaler if she needed it.

She wondered what to do next. Should she start walking to the nearest town, wherever that was? Or should she wait where she was to be rescued. After all, the wizard wouldn't leave her here forever, would he? And what about Miss Denton? Wouldn't she start worrying about where Jules had got to?

A wailing sound startled Jules and she flung herself further down into the flowers, trying to hide. The noise seemed to be getting closer. It was a thin, reedy sort of a sound and it seemed to echo around the trees. To Jules it sounded like a ghost or at least what she imagined a ghost would sound like. She tried to bury herself even deeper in the vegetation.

The sound came nearer. As well as the wailing there was a heavier sound rattling towards her. "Ghosts in chains!" she thought, terrified. The sound came even nearer. She couldn't bear to look - but then she couldn't bear not to look, either.

She raised her head a little, so she could see what had entered the clearing. It was a small, white horse or pony. It had its back to her and as it moved she realised the clanking sound was coming from a heavy metal trap that the poor creature was dragging along with it. Its hind leg was caught in the spikes of the trap and the wailing sound was its cry of distress.

"Oh, you poor thing," said Jules, standing up and moving towards the animal. "That must hurt terribly."

"It does," wailed the pony, turning its head to look at her. In the middle of its forehead was one, long spiralling horn.

Jules was speechless. This was a unicorn. A real, live unicorn and it had spoken to her, or had she just imagined it?

"Excuse me," said Jules, "but are you real?"

"Yes," said the unicorn, "are you?"

"Yes," said Jules, "I think so." It had, after all, been a very strange morning. She found it astonishing that the unicorn could talk, but she didn't like to mention it, in case the creature thought she was being rude.

"What are you doing here?" she asked.

"Trying to find somewhere to hide from the hunter," replied the unicorn. "He set this trap for me and soon he'll come to see if he's caught me."

"Why does he want to catch you?" asked Jules.

"To kill me, of course, and cut off my horn," said the unicorn, sorrowfully. "My parents warned me this would happen, but I wouldn't listen. I thought humans would be friendly, but they're not. They've killed my parents, they've killed all the other unicorns and now they're trying to kill me."

"You mean, you're the last one?" said Jules.

The unicorn nodded sadly. "I think so. I was the youngest, you see. Not much more than a baby, as unicorns go. We can live for hundreds of years, you know."

"No, I didn't," said Jules apologetically. "I don't know anything about unicorns."

The unicorn looked disappointed but carried on telling its story. "It's easy to hide when you're small, you see, but now I'm getting bigger. The hunter has spotted me and set this trap...and it hurts."

The creature's eyes filled up with tears and Jules could see blood oozing down his leg where the trap was cutting into the flesh.

"Soon he'll be along to kill me and take my horn," gulped the unicorn.

"What does he want that for?" asked Jules crouching down next to the trap.

"Humans think that a unicorn's horn is magical. They grind it up to put in medicine to make sick people better, but it doesn't work. Our magic dies with us. We can't save ourselves, let alone humans."

"Then I'll save you," said Jules firmly. "Hold still and I'll try and get you out of this trap."

Jules took a piece of fallen branch from the ground and used it to prise the jaws of the trap apart so that the young unicorn could pull its leg out. Once it was free Jules dropped the stick and the trap snapped shut, bloodstained but empty.

Jules turned and examined the unicorn. The teeth of the trap had cut deeply into the leg, which was swollen and bleeding.

"Oh dear," said Jules. "You won't be able to run far with a leg like that. Hide over there behind those trees and if the hunter comes I'll find a way to distract him."

Jules watched the unicorn limp painfully out of the clearing. Even injured, it was a beautiful creature. Its coat was brilliant white, its mane and tail a silky silver and its horn golden.

"A talking unicorn!" thought Jules, as it disappeared into the forest. "It's amazing. I thought they were extinct, if they ever existed at all. Come to think of it, aren't unicorns supposed to be mythical? Just made-up creatures? So what is it doing here? And how come it can talk?"

Jules might have stood wondering about the unicorn for some time, but her thoughts were abruptly interrupted.

"What are you doing here?" said a harsh voice. Jules spun round to see a man standing behind her. He was dressed in a tunic, belted at the waist and from the belt hung strips of different types of fur. His feet were booted, a short hooded cape covered his shoulders and his face was twisted into a scowl. Jules felt sure that this was the hunter that the unicorn had told her about. What she didn't understand was why he was wearing such strange clothing. Was he on his way to a fancy dress party? Or was that what people wore here? In that case, Jules thought the box must have taken her to a completely different part of the world. She was so busy staring at him that she forgot to reply to his question.

"What are you doing here?" the man repeated, now almost shouting.

"Just exploring," answered Jules. "I'm not doing any harm."

"Well, I don't like people 'exploring' in my part of the forest," growled the man, "so get out and don't let me catch you here again."

Jules was nervous but she wanted to give the unicorn time to get as far away as possible, so she decided to stay put and try to find out a bit more.

"Your part of the forest? Do you own it then?" she asked.

"Don't be daft, child, the king owns it, same as he owns all the forests," said the hunter, surprised.

"Which king?" said Jules, puzzled.

"King John, of course," he replied, "you must be soft in the head not to know that."

King John? Now Jules was feeling really confused, but she didn't have time to think about what it meant, because the man reached forward and grabbed her arm. He twisted it until she yelped with pain.

"I told you to get out, child. I'm not having you poaching in this forest. Anything that gets killed round here gets killed by me, get it?"

"What for?" asked Jules, trying to sound brave. "To eat?"

"Sometimes, not that it's any of your business. Mostly to sell, that's how I make my living...but sometimes for sport. You can never get enough practice at killing things."

"But that's horrible!" protested Jules. "It's cruel, like that nasty trap you set." She knew she shouldn't have mentioned the trap as soon as she said it. The hunter twisted her arm even harder and glanced round, catching sight of the trap.

"You found my trap? What was in it?"

"Nothing."

The hunter dragged Jules across the clearing to the trap. "Nothing now," he agreed, "but I caught something in it alright. The trap's not where I left it and it's been sprung. There's fresh blood on it, too. Where did the animal go?"

Just then, they heard the sound of singing coming towards them and a few moments later a young woman walked into the clearing. She wore a long dress, which reached right down to her sandaled feet. The sleeves were long too and close fitting. There was a belt round her waist and a veil, held in place by a circlet, covered her hair. In one hand she carried a metal flask and in the other a small bundle. She was still singing, a pretty, gentle melody, as she entered the clearing.

The hunter released Jules' arm and she fell to the ground. As he turned his attention to the young woman, Jules wondered about escaping from the clearing. The trouble was, the box the wizard had given her was some distance away where she'd left it when she saw the unicorn. While she wasn't sure quite what it did, she thought it might be able to help her get home, after all it got her here in the first place. Anyway it was the only chance she had, so she couldn't just run off and leave it.

Meanwhile the hunter was addressing the young woman.

"I know your tricks," he snarled. "I know what you're after. You're trying to catch my unicorn, aren't you? Everyone knows that a unicorn will come out of hiding if it hears a young girl singing."

"Why shouldn't I call it if it will come to me?" said the girl, puzzled.

"Because there's only room for one hunter in this forest and that's me. I intend to catch this unicorn and you're going to help me. Sing...sing loudly. Get the beast to come to you, then it will be an easy target. I can kill it before it realises the danger it's in."

"No," said the girl. "I'm not calling for you to hurt it. I just need its help."

"I'm the one who needs help," said the hunter, "your help. I need to catch the creature. If I can kill the last unicorn, I'll be the most famous hunter of all time and I'll make a fortune when I sell the horn." He leaned towards the young woman and added, "I'll give you a groat or two for your help."

"You can keep your coins," said the girl, "you'll get no help from me." She turned and left the clearing.

"I don't need your help," the hunter called after her, "or yours," he added turning back to Jules. "The creature must be badly injured, it can't have gone far. I'll find it soon enough." He strode out of the clearing looking for signs that would tell him which way the unicorn had gone. Fortunately, he started off in the opposite direction to the path the animal had actually taken. Once he was out of sight Jules stood up and walked over to collect the box.

Her mind was racing, trying to make sense of everything that had just happened and what the hunter had said. She was beginning to think that she wasn't in a different country after all. Could she possibly be in a different time?

"King John," she thought, trying to remember. "He ruled in...in...well, I can't remember the date, but it was centuries ago. I must be in the past and that would account for the clothes they were wearing too. So this box," she thought, turning it round in her hands, "this must have brought me here, like some sort of time machine."

She wondered if the box could take her home just as quickly but then, if it did, she wouldn't be able to help the unicorn.

"Perhaps," she thought, "I can use the box to save the unicorn. Perhaps I could find a safer time for it to live in. If it stays here the hunter is bound to find it and kill it and if I took it to my own time it would get prodded and poked about by scientists and be in all the newspapers. I don't think it would like that either. There must be a safe time for it to live in. Maybe that's the test the wizard set for me...to find a safe time for the unicorn!"

Jules went to find the unicorn. It hadn't got very far, but had managed to push its way into a clump of bushes so it couldn't be seen too easily. She explained what she was planning to do and the unicorn nodded gratefully.

"I'll be as quick as I can," said Jules. "Once I've found somewhere safe I'll come back and take you there."

"Thank you so much," replied the unicorn. "I'll wait here for you. I wouldn't be able to go far anyway, not like this."

"Try to stay out of sight," said Jules. "I'll be back soon."

Jules crawled out of the bushes and stood up. She looked at the box in her hands, wondering if there was any way to control what time it sent you to. There didn't seem to be any controls at all, so she just opened the lid.

The grey mist in the box began to emerge again, this time looking smooth and rounded like pebbles. Jules snapped the box shut and looked up.

She had changed times again. This time though she managed not to scream, she started coughing instead.

Discussion points

1. Why does Juliette want to save the unicorn?

Is it all right to only protect cute animals?

2. Is trapping animals a good way to kill them and do some animals need

to be killed?

Activity

Ask the members of the group to each think of an animal and then try to reproduce the sounds it makes. (For the sake of your eardrums, explain that accuracy is more important than volume.) Pick one or two pupils to demonstrate their animals sounds to the others.

Animal Pairs Game

The idea of this game is to get the pupils to think about how it feels to be an endangered animal, unable to find others of the same species. However, the pupils must not realise this until after the game has been played.

First explain to the whole group that you are about to play a game in which they all have to act like, and sound like, certain animals. (For older pupils who would feel embarrassed about acting like animals, you could suggest they just make the appropriate sounds.)

Tell them that you will set a specific animal for each of them to be and they will then have to move around the room as that animal, trying to recognise and join up with other animals of the same type. When they think they have collected together all the other animals of the same type, they can move to the edge of the room and sit down. Split the pupils into two roughly even-sized groups and send these groups to opposite ends of the room. Go to the first group and give each of them a specific animal to be. These are our suggestions but feel free to invent your own:

Common	(Most of the group should be given these names)
	Frog, donkey, snake, duck.
Rare	(Only a couple of people should be given these)
	Elephant, tiger.
Almost extinct	(Only one person in the whole class should be told that they are one of these)
	Gorilla, rhino, eagle, bat.

Go to the other group and repeat the process of giving them animals to represent, making sure you don't use any of the "almost extinct" animals more than once.

This will give you a mixture of animals as follows:

For example, in a class of 32 you would have approximately:

6 frogs	6 donkeys	6 snakes	6 ducks
2 elephants	2 tigers		
1 gorilla	1 rhino	1 eagle	1 bat

Tell the two groups to move into the middle of the room as the animals they are representing, then give them a couple of minutes to try and sort themselves into groups.

Stop the game when only half a dozen or so are left in the middle of the room, still searching for partners. Tell them to sit down where they are.

Go to each of the larger groups first, ask what animal they are and whether they found it easy to find others of the same type. Then speak to the small group or those in pairs and ask the same question. Lastly, go to those who didn't find partners. Ask how they felt:

Had they started to worry when they couldn't find a partner?

Had they started to realise that there might not be another animal of their type?

Give them a chance to say how they felt, then explain that you had only given out one of certain animals. Point out to everyone that how these few pupils felt would be a little like how it would feel to be an endangered animal. You don't know you're rare because you've seen it in a documentary or read it in a book. All you know is that you're looking and looking for others of the same kind and you can't find them. Imagine how that feels.

That is how the unicorn in the story is feeling!

The Last Unicorn: Lesson 2 Worksheet

Companionship

How much do we take the company of others for granted? How would we feel if we were alone and couldn't find other people?

For some animals it's harder than others. Animals who normally live alone, covering a large territory, would find it easier than those which usually live in groups or cramped in a confined area. Remember that animals who live alone will still find partners to breed and have young from time to time.

Look at the following list of animals:

Rabbits, tigers, bats, elephants, badgers, jaguars, wolves, Mountain lions (Pumas), Polar bears, zebras, moles and chimpanzees.

Place them in whichever of the following categories you feel they belong:

Live alone   **Live in groups**

_____

_____

_____

_____

_____

_____

_____

The Last Unicorn: Lesson 2 Worksheet continued

Companionship

The sociable animals would find it harder to be alone, but eventually even the most solitary animal would have to go looking for a mate and keep looking for one, even if there were none left to find.

Which words would you use to describe how you would feel if you were cut off from other humans?

_____

_____

_____

_____

_____

_____

Lesson 3

Jules makes a new friend and realises that her task will not be easy

Recap

Question: How did Jules discover where she was?

Answer: By talking to the hunter.

Question: What did she discover in the forest?

Answer: A unicorn.

Question: Why did she decide to help the unicorn?

Answer: Because she felt sorry for it.

Jules was surrounded by smoke. She thought some of the mist from the box must have escaped, but when she glanced down she saw that the lid of the box was shut. Her chest was feeling very tight, so she reached into her pocket, pulled out her inhaler and took a couple of doses. Her breathing began to ease a little. Jules turned round and found the wizard standing behind her. She nearly jumped out of her skin.

"What are you doing here?" she asked.

"More to the point, young lady, what are you doing here?" said the wizard. "This isn't where I sent you."

"I'm just trying to do what you wanted me to," Jules said defiantly.

"Really?" replied the wizard. "And what was that?"

"Find a safe place for the unicorn," she answered impatiently. "Have you come to help me?"

"Yes," said the wizard, "and no."

"What kind of answer is that?"

"I can't give you too much help, can I? It is you who's supposed to be taking the test, not me... but I can offer you one word of warning before you try any more trips through time."

"What?" Jules asked curiously.

"Think of a fairy tale," replied the wizard mysteriously, then he disappeared completely. It seemed to happen instantly. Jules reached out her hand to where he had been standing. Perhaps he was still there and she just couldn't see him...but her hand just felt the empty air. He really was gone.

"Oh no," thought Jules miserably, "now I'm alone again. There are so many things I should have asked him, like how do I get home?"

Jules realised that she'd just have to keep trying to work things out for herself. She began to look around to see where the box had brought her to this time.

The trees were gone and she was in a dirty, smoky town. The streets were cobbled and the tall buildings were streaked with grime. Smart carriages pulled by horses moved briskly along, while street vendors moved up and down the pavement trying to sell flowers and pies to the people passing by.

The damp air, heavy with smoke, curled round Jules, and she had to use her inhaler again. She felt helpless, uncertain where to start. Then she saw a boy, a couple of years older than she was, who appeared to be brushing the road. She went over to him to try and find out where or when she was, but before she could even say hello the boy started to laugh at her.

"Cor blimey, mate, where'd you get that clobber?" he asked.

"Clobber?" said Jules, puzzled. "What do you mean?"

"Your clothes, of course. I've not seen anyone wearing stuff like that before."

"What's wrong with my clothes?" she asked.

"I didn't say there was anything wrong with them. They're just a bit strange, that's all." He grinned at her.

"No they're not," said Jules, indignantly. "They're no stranger than yours, anyway."

"Here, there's nothing wrong with mine," said the boy. He straightened up, trying to brush the dirt off his ragged trousers. Jules saw that his feet were bare and his shirt, which was too small for him, had holes in it. "Nothing that a few patches here and there wouldn't fix, anyway," he continued. He turned away and went back to his sweeping.

"What are you doing?" asked Jules curiously.

"What does it look like? I'm sweeping the road. I'm a crossing-sweeper, I am. I sweeps all the mud and such off the cobbles so that people can cross the road without getting their feet all filthy and they pay me for it."

"Where I come from the streets are much cleaner," said Jules, feeling smug until honesty forced her to add, "except for the litter."

"And where do you come from then?"

"From the future."

She was about to explain when the road sweeper interrupted her saying, "The future?"

"I think so," said Jules. "What year are we in?"

"What do you mean, what year?" said the boy.

Jules, inspired by her last encounter with somebody from a different time, asked, "Who's king at the moment?"

"King?" said the boy amazed. "We don't have no king no more. We've got Queen Victoria."

"You're a Victorian?" said Jules, pleased to have reached a time she had some knowledge of.

"Who are you calling names?" said the boy, offended.

"All I meant was, you're someone who lived..." she corrected herself, "lives during the reign of Queen Victoria... Victorian, see?"

"I suppose so," he said grudgingly. "But just you watch your lip. I'm not having no-one calling me names, especially a lunatic like you."

"I'm not a lunatic."

"Yes, you are," grinned the boy. "Saying you're from the future. That's rubbish, that is."

"No, it's not."

"How did you get here then?"

"With this time machine," said Jules, pointing at the carved wooden box. The boy laughed.

"That's not a machine," he said, "it's just a box. I've seen machines. They're great big metal things in factories, all cogs and wheels and things. You'd never fit one into that little box and, even if you did, it couldn't move you through time."

"It could," said Jules, crossly. "It did!"

"Why?" asked the boy suddenly. "Why would anyone want to go hopping through time, anyway?"

"If you must know," Jules said importantly, "I'm trying to find a safe place to put a unicorn."

If she was expecting him to be impressed, she was disappointed. The boy just looked at her blankly and asked, "What's a unicorn?"

"You must know that," said Jules shocked. "Everyone knows that."

"Well, I don't," said the boy, defensively.

"Why not?" asked Jules.

"'Cos there's lots of things I don't know. I've never been to school or nothing, never had time. When I was a nipper I helped me granddad. He used to grow vegetables and bring them into town to sell. When he died I was too young to work the place on me own. Anyway, the landlord wouldn't let me so I ended up here, got meself a brush and started to make me own way in the world. Now, are you going to tell me what a whatsicorn is or ain't you?"

"It's a sort of a horse, but with a long, thin horn in the middle of its forehead."

"Cows have horns, not horses."

"That's why it's special," said Jules triumphantly. "And it's the very last one!"

"Well, whatever it is," said the boy, "I wouldn't bring it here."

"Why not?"

"If it's some kind of a horse it'll need grass or summat to eat. There's none of that round here. You're in the middle of a town. You'd do better to take it out into the country."

"I suppose so," said Jules uncertainly, beginning to realise that there were a lot of things about the unicorn she didn't know. Things she probably needed to know if she was going to find the right place for it.

"I'm not really sure what the poor thing needs," she admitted guiltily.

"Then why don't you ask someone who does know? There's a professor who lives over there," the boy said, pointing to a house further down the street. "I've heard he knows ever such a lot about animals."

"Alright," Jules agreed. "I'll ask him...but will you come with me, introduce me to him?" She was feeling nervous about having to talk to yet another stranger and a professor at that.

"Why should I?" the boy replied. "I've got work to do. I run a few errands for the grocer when he's busy and he said I could earn a penny or two today if I'm willing to do a few hours work."

"Only a penny or two, for hours of work?" questioned Jules, horrified.

The boy looked puzzled. "It's fair enough and better than some pay."

"But what can you buy with a penny? Where I come from that would hardly buy you a sweet."

"Well, I can get a bite of food for it or a place to stay for the night so I'm not complaining," the boy answered, "but I'd better get there quick or someone else will get the work." He slung his brush over his shoulder and walked away.

She watched him go, wondering what it would be like not to know where you were going to sleep at night or when you'd next have the money for a meal. She hoped the grocer would have some work for him. Then she realised that if she couldn't work out how to get home, she might be in the same position herself. She hurried towards the professor's house.

She was about to ring the doorbell when a well-dressed, elderly gentleman walked up the steps to the door and put his key in the lock.

"Excuse me," Jules said nervously. "Are you the professor?"

"That's right young lady," he replied, looking her up and down clearly surprised at Jules clothing. "How can I help you?"

"I had a question I wanted to ask you about an animal," said Jules, pleased to meet someone who seemed both able and willing to help her.

"Then you've come to the right place. I know everything there is to know about animals. You should see my collection," he said proudly.

"You keep animals?"

"Oh yes, all sorts. They're all over the house, hundreds of them."

"Doesn't that get a bit messy?" asked Jules, picturing wild animals of all kinds roaming through every room.

"Oh no," said the professor, "my housekeeper dusts them regularly."

"Dusts them?" said Jules, confused. She tried to imagine his housekeeper reaching up to dust behind an elephant's ears while the creature swung its trunk around, knocking over ornaments.

"Surely it takes more than a duster to clean up after that many animals?" she said, thinking that a wheelbarrow and shovel would be more use.

"You really are a strange girl," said the professor. "Is that your question?"

"No, sorry" said Jules, worried that the first person who could help her might begin to run out of patience. "I wanted to ask you what you would do if you found something like a unicorn I mean, where would you put it?"

"Right above the mantelpiece," said the professor decidedly. "In pride of place just above the fire."

"Wouldn't it get a bit hot there?" questioned Jules.

"Does it matter? It's not as if it would be able to feel anything, not once it was stuffed." The professor swung the door of the house open, so Jules could see into his hallway. The heads of various animals were mounted all round the walls, their glass eyes staring back at her. He went and stood next to the head of an enormous moose, stroking its neck affectionately.

"Stuffed!" echoed Jules, shocked.

"Of course they're stuffed," he continued. "You didn't think I kept live animals, did you? Everything in my collection is dead and filled with sawdust." He added proudly, "I've got some of the rarest animals in the world in my collection. Always make a point of killing animals before they die out."

"You kill them?" said Jules, horrified. She stepped into the hall - the whole place smelt like death.

"That's right."

"But if an animal's rare, if there are only a few left and you kill one for your collection, the animal becomes even rarer."

"Precisely," said the professor, "that's why I have to get my specimens before there are none left to collect."

"You're no better than the hunter I met earlier," said Jules, appalled. "You don't care about the animals, you just care about collecting them, building up a complete set. I bet you don't know anything at all about what animals need while they're alive!" She turned and ran for the door.

"Why should I?" the professor shouted after her, "that stage of their life cycle doesn't interest me at all."

"Then there's no point in asking you any more questions about my unicorn because you won't know the answers." Jules was furious, she felt betrayed by the one person who had given her a glimmer of hope.

"There's no such thing as unicorns, you know," the professor said, patronisingly. "They're just legends… myths… stories made up by ignorant, unscientific people or silly children like you."

Jules fled the professor's house close to tears, not even stopping to shut the door behind her. She ran around the corner so the house was out of sight and sank to her knees. The professor hadn't helped her at all. She still didn't know what the unicorn needed and she was beginning to get tired and hungry herself. Suddenly the whole situation felt helpless. She knelt on the cold cobbles and began to cry. "I might as well just give up," she snivelled to herself as she cradled the wooden box on her lap.

"Here, you don't want to go doing that," said a voice from beside her. "Giving up never solved nothing for nobody. You got to keep on trying." Jules looked up. It was the boy she'd been talking to earlier, the road-sweeper. He carried on talking, "Take me, you see. I got to the grocers to find he'd given my work to another boy, but I ain't just giving up. I've come back here to try and earn some money road sweeping. And that's what you need to do. Have another bash at helping that unithingy of yours."

"Thanks," said Jules, "but I don't know how." She started to cry again.

"Don't go getting all sniffly on me. Here, you can use me hanky, if you like".

Jules took the ragged handkerchief the boy offered her and wiped her eyes with it before handing it back to him.

"Thanks," she said embarrassed. "I don't even know your name."

"I'm Bert."

"I'm called Juliette."

"Juliette? That's a bit of a mouthful, isn't it?"

"You can call me Jules, if you like."

"Alright Jules." He sat beside her on the step. "The professor couldn't help then?"

"No. He just wants to collect dead animals, not help live ones."

"Then you'd better not bring your unicorn creature here. There's lots of people like him around these days. Science, well, it's the fashion, isn't it? If he just wants the animal dead, chances are all the others will too."

"Then there's no-one who can help me," groaned Jules. She looked at Bert. "Unless you will?"

"Why should I? No-one ever helps me, so why should I help anyone?" He stood up. "Besides, you've just made the whole thing up anyway. All that stuff about being from the future, that's rubbish that is. I expect you've made up the unicorn as well."

"No, I haven't!" Jules jumped up. "And I can prove it."

"How?"

"By showing you. I'll take you back with me to see it. It's in the past, you see. The box will take us there."

"I'm not going anywhere," said Bert nervously.

"Chicken, coward… you're just frightened," chanted Jules.

"I'm not frightened of nothing, me, but I'm not going nowhere, especially with a girl."

"Suit yourself," Jules shrugged. "I don't want your help anyway. I'll just get the box to take me somewhere else."

Bert reached out to touch the box, wanting to see for himself how something so small could be some kind of a machine.

"Don't touch it," said Jules, trying to pull it away from him. "You might break it."

"I only want to look at it," and he grabbed if off her.

"No. You don't know what it can do." Jules panicked and tried to snatch it back off Bert just as he lifted the lid, which is how they both came to be touching the box when it started to move through time.

"Oh no. Not again," thought Jules.

Bert was too surprised to think anything at all.

The mist curling out of the open box seemed to be forming itself into the image of yellowing grass, then green leaves then yellowing grass again. Jules snapped the lid shut and called out. "Bert?"

There was no sign of him. "Bert?" she shouted. "Where are you?" Then she found she couldn't shout at all. The air tasted really stale and full of fumes. Jules struggled to breathe. She pulled out her inhaler and used it hurriedly. It didn't help at all. She still couldn't breathe.

Discussion points

1. Why did Juliette have difficulty breathing in Victorian times?

2. Was there a difference between the hunter and the professor who collected animals?

Activity

Ask the group to suggest different methods of hunting, for example shooting, fishing, trapping, poisoning etc. and different tools to hunt with, for example guns, nets, bows and arrows. With younger pupils you can get them to mime these activities. Explain that people have always hunted animals - the problems start when we over-hunt and drive creatures to extinction.

Greedy Monkeys Game

This game requires about a dozen sweets. We used the candy bananas you can get from 'pick & mix' stalls. It's also useful to have a bowl to put them in.

This is a game about how people use the environment. Explain to the group that they have to imagine that the bowl of sweet bananas is actually a banana tree in a forest. They must imagine that they are a monkey that comes across the tree. They must put their hand up to tell you how many bananas they would take from the tree and why. If you accept their answer (and their reasoning) they can come and collect that number of banana sweets. They must assume the monkey only eats one banana at a time.

Possible acceptable answers:

> 1. to eat on the spot.
> 2. one for now, one for later.
> 3. one for monkey, one for its baby or family.
> 4. one for monkey, two for family etc.

Anything over three and they'd need a pretty impressive reason.

Unacceptable answers:

> 1. more than three to keep for later.

Remind them that monkeys don't have fridges. They would leave the fruit on the tree and come back to it next time it was needed.

Now ask, "Who really wanted to say they would like to take all the bananas on the tree?"

A few honest hands will go up. Explain that that's why we humans are the only 'greedy monkeys'. We're the ones who would take more than we needed at the time, or needed for our family that day. We'd pick all the fruit on the tree to sell it, leaving nothing for the other animals so there would be no bananas for tomorrow. Clear an area of its fruit too thoroughly and there might not be enough seeds left for a crop the following year either (because fruit contains the seeds of the plant it grows on).

Point out that that's why it's humans who need to change their attitude to the world. Going back to the idea of trying to save a species of animals or protect a habitat, it's not enough to just make laws banning hunting. After all, if you're told not to do something you immediately start thinking of ways to do it without getting caught!

For many people, hunting has been part of their way of life for generations and they don't see why they should stop. That's why, as well as making laws and enforcing them, the hunters have to be educated. They have to be shown why it matters that a species of animal doesn't die out. If the hunter's survival is dependent on the animals they kill, perhaps they need to be shown a different way to benefit from the animal and its habitat, for example by using the animals to encourage tourists to visit the area, which will bring money into the local economy.

Any solution that ignores the needs of the local human population won't work in the long run. The humans need to be taught to understand the situation and be equipped to change their role in it.

In the worksheet "Need versus Greed" you might feel it would be useful to have a discussion regarding the difference between needs and wants.

The Last Unicorn: Lesson 3 Worksheet

Need versus Greed

In the game we explored the idea that humans are the only "Greedy Monkeys." This worksheet is about the differences between need and want.

Tick one box that best describes each item listed:

Item	Need	Want	Item	Need	Want
Water	☐	☐	Somewhere to live	☐	☐
Television	☐	☐	Computer games	☐	☐
Clothing	☐	☐	Parks and countryside to enjoy	☐	☐
Ways to travel about	☐	☐	Entertainment	☐	☐
Computers	☐	☐	Designer label clothing	☐	☐
Pets	☐	☐	Smart ways to travel about	☐	☐
Education	☐	☐	Food e.g. vegetables, meat, fruit, bread	☐	☐
Treat food, eg. chocolate, crisps and fizzy drinks	☐	☐	Somewhere cool to live	☐	☐
Books	☐	☐	CDs	☐	☐

Wanting things you don't need doesn't make you a bad person. It just means you're human. However, it's important to understand which of these are essential and which things are luxuries which you may have to wait for or may not be in a situation to have at all. For example, you can't have a pet if you've nowhere to keep it. That doesn't mean that pets aren't important. Some people would say they need them; some people just want them; others aren't bothered if they never have any. We're all individuals. What we need to learn is that we can't have anything and everything we want if someone (or something) else has to suffer so that we can have it.

Examples

▸ Having a pet in unsuitable conditions.

▸ Having furniture made from rainforest timber instead of renewable sources.

▸ Having cheap clothing when the person across the world who makes it isn't paid enough to live on.

▸ Having cheap food now at the cost of the environment in the future.

Many of these situations aren't black and white. Answers aren't always easy, but we need to learn to be responsible about the things we want and need, and the way we learn to spend our money, whether it's a little or a lot.

What things do you think are really important in your life?

How many of them are things you own and how many, such as friendships, happen naturally? It's easy to get caught up in wanting more and more 'things' and forgetting other aspects of life.

Lesson 4

Bert and Jules get lost in time

Recap

Question: In what time did Jules find herself?

Answer: Victorian England.

Question: What did she learn from her meeting with Bert?

Answer: How difficult life could be in Victorian times.

Question: Was the professor interested in helping the unicorn?

Answer: No, he only wanted to collect dead animals.

Bert looked around nervously. Where there had been tall buildings and cobbled streets, there were now only trees, flowers and grass. There was no sign of Jules or the box they'd been arguing over. There was no sign of anything Bert recognised at all. Even his broom was gone.

"Jules," he called, "where are you? What's going on? Jules?" There was no answer. "Is this some kind of trick?" His own voice echoed back at him. He could see a narrow path leading through the trees and decided he might as well start walking. Perhaps doing something would stop him feeling so frightened.

"After all," he thought, "Jules must be around here somewhere. All I've got to do is find her then maybe she can explain what's going on," and he set off along the path.

****

Jules was terrified. More frightened than she'd ever been in her life. She really couldn't breathe the air in the place the box had brought her to. Her lungs felt like they were shutting down altogether and her inhaler wasn't helping at all.

Suddenly the wizard appeared beside her. He was holding what looked like an inhaler, but it was much larger than the one Jules was trying to use. It had something that looked like an oxygen mask attached to it. He hastily fitted the mask over her nose and mouth and showed her how to control the device. He kept talking to her too, trying to reassure her to stop her panicking.

"It's alright," he was saying, "you'll feel better in a moment or two. Then you'll just need to use it every few minutes. That's it. Breathe steadily."

Eventually Jules started to breathe more easily. After a few minutes, when she was breathing normally, the wizard eased the mask off her face.

"Better?" he asked. She nodded weakly.

"Where am I?" Jules gasped, finally able to notice where the box had transported her to this time.

They appeared to be in a park of some sort. The trees were all planted in straight lines, but were very thin and spindly. The grass around them was yellow and withered, as if it had been covered up for weeks and was only just seeing the sun again. The sky above them seemed to be hidden by a dark, grey haze, which looked more threatening than the

most thunderous raincloud. There were signs everywhere that read, "Keep off the grass - or else." Jules felt she'd never seen such an unwelcoming place. The wizard was sitting on the grass beside her, looking worried. He didn't seem to have heard her question.

"I said, where am I?" Jules repeated.

"'Where'? Don't you mean 'when'?" he asked. "You're in the future. Well, the future compared to your time, anyway."

"This is still the Earth then?"

"Oh, yes," said the wizard. "This is the Earth alright."

"Then why can't I breathe?"

"The air here is too dirty, too polluted with chemicals, but people who live here now have learned to adjust. You're just not used to it, that's all."

Jules couldn't believe that the air on earth could have got so bad. She needed to use the inhaler device every couple of minutes.

"I thought things were supposed to be better in the future. People are supposed to be looking after the environment more. How could they let this happen?"

The wizard smiled. He had been really concerned about Jules when he'd found her. He hadn't expected the girl to find it quite so difficult to breathe but now she was feeling well enough to ask questions, he felt he could relax a little. He began to tease her again.

"Don't you know?" he replied, in answer to her question. "I thought you knew about lots of things. That's what you told me when we met."

"Well, I was wrong," said Jules, sulkily.

"Good," said the wizard, smiling at her. "Realising that there are things you don't know is the first step towards learning anything."

"I suppose you do know everything," she challenged him.

"No," he replied with a grin, "but I do know rather a lot."

"Why don't you save the unicorn then?" she said huffily.

"It really isn't that simple."

"That's a typical grown-up answer."

"Really?" said the wizard. "Do I strike you as a typical grown up?"

"Not exactly," said Jules, reluctantly.

"Good! I didn't think you could be completely stupid, Jules."

"Juliette!" she snapped. "I told you, only my friends call me Jules!"

"Aren't I your friend?"

"No!"

"What?" queried the wizard, looking amazed. "I lend you my time machine, allow you to meet the rarest animal in the world, bring you a super-inhaler when you're foolish enough to jump into the future unprepared and you say I'm not your friend?"

"In other words, you got me into this mess," Jules muttered crossly, "and it's not fair. I didn't ask to come here." She was beginning to feel really tired from the asthma attack and she still didn't know how she was going to get home. The wizard could see that she was very close to tears, even though she was arguing with him. "Besides," she added, "how can we be friends? I can't even remember your name."

"Malkezawiz," he reminded her gently. "Wiz for short."

"Alright, Wiz, now what?" Jules surprised herself with the question, almost as much as she surprised the wizard, but she couldn't help it. She was beginning to realise that she couldn't solve the unicorn's problems or get herself home without help. The wizard was the only person there to ask, and in a way she trusted him. He'd sent her off on this adventure, but he'd also been there to help her when she was really in trouble. Surely he wouldn't let her down now?

"Are you asking for my help?"

"Maybe," said Jules grudgingly. After all, she didn't want to give in too easily.

"Very well," he replied, "then I suggest you carry on with what you came here to do. See if the future is a safe place to bring your unicorn."

That wasn't the answer Jules was hoping for and she was about to start arguing with him again when he vanished.

"I hate it when you do that," she shouted at the space where Wiz had been.

She looked up to see a strangely dressed man walking towards her. He was wearing a shiny silver suit, a bit like the ones Jules had seen in science fiction programmes on television. She scrambled to her feet, taking another dose from the super-inhaler.

By now the man had nearly reached her and she could see his face was sharp and suspicious. "Where are your papers?" he demanded.

Jules was puzzled, "What papers?"

"Everyone has papers."

"I must have lost them," she said quickly.

"You're not allowed to enter the national wilderness without permission. I need to inspect your papers. Make sure you've got the proper permits."

"This is a wilderness?" queried Jules, amazed. "It looks more like a city park."

"This is the last great wilderness," said the man proudly. "Only licensed hunters come here."

"Hunters?" Jules repeated, disappointed. She'd thought that people in the future would be better about protecting wildlife but it seemed that they weren't. "What do you find to hunt in such a tame-looking place?"

"Cats," said the man in hushed tones.

"Cats?"

"Wild ones," the man continued. "That's just about all there is left to hunt these days."

"You don't have to be terribly brave to hunt cats," said Jules, scornfully.

"Yes, you do," he said, defensively. "You can get a nasty scratch from a pussy cat, you know. You have to be very brave to kill a cat."

"But why would you want to?" Jules was struggling to understand this strange man. "Do you need them for food?"

"Don't be disgusting," he answered. "Nobody would dream of actually eating them."

"Then I don't understand… are there too many of them?" Jules persisted.

"Oh no. There's hardly any left now. That's why you have to have a licence to hunt them."

"Then what do you kill them for? Is it their fur? Do you wear it?" Jules was determined to find out why he was so keen on hunting.

"Do I look like someone with such dreadful taste in clothes?" said the man, offended. "Fur against the skin, ugh! How primitive! Although it is rather impressive to have a few pelts on one's belt, don't you think?"

Jules saw that he had some strips of animal fur tied to his belt, just like the first hunter she had met - but amongst these furs were tiger and leopard and other rare animals. Jules was furious.

"I think it's disgusting. You're just killing for the sake of it. You're as bad as the hunter and the professor I met earlier. Haven't you learned anything from the past at all? Can't you see what you and your kind of people are doing to the world? You're destroying it."

"Don't be ridiculous," he said, unable to see what she was making such a fuss about.

"What will you do when you've run out of cats to hunt?" she asked.

"Pick a different animal," said the man calmly. "The sport must go on."

"But it's not a sport, not for the animals. It's life and death to them."

By now Jules was almost shouting, but he just ignored her and carried on talking.

"Next on the list, once we've run out of cats will be mice. It'll have to be, with no cats to control them. I'd prefer hedgehogs myself. There's more sport to hunting hedgehogs or squirrels… "

He drifted off into his own little world, picturing himself as the brave hunter, risking life and limb in the eternal struggle to kill small furry animals.

Jules demanded his attention asking, "Are there lots of people like you round here?"

"Oh yes," he said enthusiastically. "Hunting's very popular these days, now everyone's got so much free time." Suddenly he turned, pointing to a clump of bushes. "Look over there… " he whispered. A black and white cat was staring at them as it crouched in the shadows. The hunter started to move slowly towards the cat, creeping up on it. The cat's tail began to twitch. Jules watched, horrified, as the man got closer and closer. The hunter pulled a net out of his pocket and tried to manoeuvre it so that he could fling it over the animal, trapping it before he moved in for the kill.

Just as Jules thought the cat had no chance of escape it leapt forward, jumping up to claw the man's hand. He cursed and dropped the net as the cat ran off across the park. The hunter chased after the animal, but it was obvious he wouldn't be able to catch it. The cat had too much of a head start.

Jules turned away, relieved the cat had escaped, but with a new concern – what was she supposed to do now? It was obvious she couldn't bring the unicorn here. "The future seems as dangerous as the past," she thought. She picked up the box, wondering where it would take her next. She opened the lid but nothing happened. Nothing at all. The grey mist inside the box just stayed there. It didn't change shape or colour, it just hung there, like a tiny storm cloud. The time machine either wasn't working or worse still, it was broken.

****

Bert was wandering round in circles. It's easy to do when you're lost and Bert was very lost. He was also beginning to get really scared. Usually, nothing scared Bert. He was used to trouble, to being shouted at and getting the odd kick. He was used to fending for himself too and finding his own food and shelter. That was the kind of trouble he could deal with. This was different, wandering round and round what seemed to be an enormous wood, trying to find a girl he hardly knew so he could get home.

"Home," he thought miserably, "not that I've had much of a home since me granddad died. Those were the best times, working in the countryside with him. I've always liked the countryside." He glanced round at the dense woodland and added out loud, "but I'm not too stuck on this bit." He trudged on.

****

Jules shut the lid of the box and wondered what to do next. She didn't want to be trapped here, of all places. "Wiz," she called out. "Wiz, please, where are you? I need your help."

The wizard suddenly appeared in front of her, making her jump. He smiled saying, "You called? What's the matter?" Jules glared at him. She really didn't like the way he could just vanish and reappear like that. It was unnerving.

"Your stupid time machine has stopped working," she complained.

"No, it hasn't."

"Well it's broken then."

"That is also incorrect. You've used up all your journeys, that's all." Jules looked at him blankly. "I did warn you," Wiz explained. "I told you to think about fairy tales."

"Fairy tales?" Jules was bewildered. "What have fairy tales got to do with anything?"

"Think, Juliette, think," said Wiz. "You don't really imagine that an ordinary human child could be allowed unlimited travel through time, do you? Everything has limits."

"I don't understand," wailed Jules, frustrated and at the limit of her patience.

"I tried to warn you," Wiz continued. "I thought you'd understand. After all, everyone knows how many wishes you get in fairy tales."

"Three," Jules answered.

"Exactly, but why?"

"Because well, because that's the way it is in fairy tales," said Jules.

"Unfortunately, that's also the way it is in time travel."

"So," said Jules slowly, thinking it through, "I can only use the box three times."

"That's right. You've had your three trips, Juliette."

"You mean I'm stuck here forever?" she asked in a very small voice.

"Theoretically, yes, but I think there may be a solution if we bend the rules a little," said Wiz. "All you have to do is get somebody who still has some time journeys left to allow you to use theirs."

"Who? You?" asked Jules hopefully.

"Why should I help you?" said Wiz. "We're not friends, remember? That's why I have to keep calling you Juliette."

Jules smiled sweetly at him and said, "You can call me Jules, if you like."

Wiz wasn't fooled. "No, you're not saying that because we're friends, but because you want something from me. That doesn't count."

"But you will help me?" pleaded Jules.

"I can't give you any time journeys. The machine doesn't work for me," said the wizard, adding mysteriously, "I have… other ways of getting about."

He looked at Jules' disappointed face and put a reassuring arm around her shoulders. "It's alright. I know somebody who can help."

"Who?" asked Jules trying not to feel too hopeful.

"Bert, of course," said Wiz.

"Bert?" Jules realised guiltily that she hadn't thought about the boy since she arrived in the future.

How could she have forgotten all about him like that? She tried to concentrate on what Wiz was telling her.

"You were both touching the time machine at the start of your last journey", he was saying. "When you shot into the future he was thrown into the opposite direction, which means he's trapped in the past. The difference is he's only had one time journey, so he's allowed two more. I'm sure he won't mind if you use one of his remaining trips to take the time machine back to him. Then he'll have one journey left. He can use it to get back to his time, or give it to you to get back to yours. It'll be his decision."

Wiz held his hand over the box Jules was holding. The patterns flowing across his robe seemed to float along his arm and gather over the box. Leaves formed in the air above the box. The lid sprang open and the mist in it shot up to join the pattern already hanging in the air. Then the whole mass sank back into the box and the lid slapped shut. Almost instantly, they were back in the past, in the forest where Jules had found the unicorn.

Discussion points

1. Why couldn't Juliette breathe in the future?

2. Is hunting animals a sport?

Activity

Explain the world habitat if the pupils are unfamiliar with it. (The place where an animal lives, characterised by its physical and living properties, for example a rain forest is characterised by its vegetation and its climate.)

Tree Life Game

Obviously one of the best ways to protect an animal is to protect the habitat where it lives. Some areas are turned into nature reserves or national parks, where hunting and development are forbidden. Getting the balance right here too can be difficult.

Get the pupils to form a large circle. This represents a protected area of habitat. Ask for 4 volunteers to step into the circle to represent 4 clumps of trees. Each clump of trees can support one family of monkeys, providing them with shelter, food etc. Choose 4 more volunteers each to represent a family of monkeys and send them each to join a different clump of trees. Point out that this balance could be sustained for some time. Ask the pupils what could happen to change the balance.

Possibilities

1. Due to development, animals from other areas enter the protected area. This results in greater competition as the habitat can only support the number of animals already there. Therefore, either the incoming animals or some of the resident animals will die out due to lack of food etc. Demonstrate this by having another volunteer enter the circle. Let the group decide if the new group of animals is going to die or one of the ones already there. Whoever dies lies on the floor while the survivors take up positions by the trees.

2. The resident animals will breed, increasing the population, but there is not enough forest to support them and due to development all round them, they cannot move on to find territories of their own. Add in 4 more volunteers to represent the additional animals. Let the group choose who is going to die, young or old. The 4 clumps of trees can still only support the same number of animals as before.

3. Local hunters will know that that it the best place to hunt because all the animals are in that protected habitat instead of being spread out over a wider area. This makes hunting easy, even if it's illegal. Pick one volunteer to come in as the hunter. This person has to move round the animals as fast as possible, tapping them on the shoulder to indicate he's killed them. (The population will be extinct in seconds.)

Point out that for a protected area to be effective it has to be saved early enough that there is still a sufficient amount of land to support a large number of animals across a range of species. The land itself may need to be managed to prevent overcrowding and occasionally animals may need to be moved to other sites. Also, it's not enough to make hunting illegal, the area has to be policed to deter or catch the hunter.

The Last Unicorn : Lesson 4 Worksheet

Habitats

For a habitat to work properly it needs a range of different organisms interacting together. Even a habitat as simple as a meadow can be complex:

To turn sunlight into energy for growth we need **p**_ _ _ _ _.

These provide food for plant eating animals such as _ _ **w** _ .

The waste from these animals falls to the ground and is broken down by

_ _ _ **r o** _ _ _ to act as fertiliser, enriching the _ _ **i** _.

Insect numbers are controlled by _ _ _ **d** _ who eat them in the daylight and **b** _ _ _

who feed on them at night.

Both plants and animals need a supply of _ _ **t** _ _.

If you were trying to manage the habitat looked at in the game, what methods would you use to deal with the problems that cropped up?

Overcrowding as other animals moved into the area or new ones were born:

_____

_____

To allow natural movements of animals between sites, it is becoming more common to leave wildlife corridors. What do you think a wildlife corridor is?

_____

_____

How would you deal with the problem of hunting?

_____

_____

How difficult would it be to make your solutions work in practice? Would you need a large team of people to help you? Where might you get the money from to pay this team?

_____

_____

There are no cheap or easy solutions.

Lesson 5

Jules discovers that even in the past you can be too late

Recap

Question: What was the air like in the future?

Answer: Very polluted and almost unbreathable.

Question: Had people learned from the lessons of the past?

Answer: No. They were still hunting animals and polluting the air.

Question: What did Jules discover when she tried to leave the future?

Answer: She'd used up all her journeys.

Jules breathed the clean air with relief. She and Wiz were standing in the clearing where she'd first seen the unicorn. The trap was still there but there was no sign of the creature that had been caught in it. Jules led Wiz over to the clump of bushes where the unicorn had been hiding, saying, "I told it to wait here for me." The unicorn wasn't there either.

"Where is it?" asked Jules. "And where's Bert? I thought the box was supposed to take us to him."

"He'll be here somewhere," Wiz answered. "You just have to find him."

Jules glanced round the vast forest. All she could see, in any direction, were trees. "How can I? I don't know my way around here so I'll never be able to find him or the unicorn." She sat on a fallen tree trunk, her shoulders slumped in defeat. "Not that it matters," she added, "I didn't find a way to save it anyway. You were right, Wiz, I don't know enough about history to know what time I should have taken the unicorn to."

Wiz sat beside her. "Perhaps not," he said kindly, "but at least you realise that now. And you do know about other things."

"Like what?"

"Well, you said you knew lots about the environment. Maybe you could have used some of your ideas about that to save the unicorn. What do you think people would do to protect a wild animal in your own time?"

"I suppose," said Jules, considering it for the first time, "they might take the unicorn and put it in a zoo, to keep it safe." She sat up straighter, getting excited about the idea. "Yes, that's it. We could build a zoo, a safe place for all the animals that are dying out. We could have the unicorn in it and rare animals like Giant pandas and Mountain gorillas. We could keep them all safe. We could even go and collect creatures that have died out in the past like the Dodo! Can we do it Wiz, please?"

"Jules, you don't know enough about any of these animals to look after them properly."

"Yes, I do!" Jules said indignantly.

"Really?" questioned Wiz. "Can you even tell me what any of them eat?"

Jules was silent. She hadn't a clue about what to feed any of them. Wiz saw how disappointed she looked and said, "The idea of a zoo as a safe place for rare animals is a good one, but you can't go hopping around through time to collect them. You've used up all your time journeys, remember?" Jules nodded, gloomily. "You really ought to go and find Bert, to give him the box. That is why you came back here."

"I suppose so," said Jules, standing up. She added nervously, "Wiz, if he doesn't let me have his journey home and I'm stuck here in the past, will you come and visit me sometimes?"

"Would you want me to?"

"Yes, I think so I'd be frightened and lonely, I'd need a friend."

"Then of course I'll visit you, Jules."

"Thanks, Wiz," she smiled at him. "Are you sure the zoo idea wouldn't work? For the unicorn, I mean? Couldn't you take it to a zoo somewhere?"

Wiz looked at Jules' hopeful face and felt guilty. He knew it was time to tell her that it was too late to save the unicorn. Putting one animal in a zoo might keep it safe, but you needed two animals, or more, if you were going to save the species. Once you were down to the last animal, like the unicorn, it was too late. It was bound to die eventually and there would be no more to replace it. Unicorns would be gone forever and nothing could bring them back.

Jules was still smiling at him, waiting for an answer.

"Just go and find Bert," he said.

****

Bert was still searching through the woods trying to find Jules. He was beginning to think he'd be stuck there forever and the idea terrified him. To keep himself calm he kept repeating, "I ain't scared of nothing, me," but it wasn't working. He was scared.

It felt like he'd been searching for hours when he finally found something, but it wasn't Jules. It was the body of a silvery white horse, lying dead among the trees. Bert knew it must be Jules' unicorn because there was the stump of a horn sticking out from its forehead. The rest of the horn had been sawn off and taken away. The hunter had finally caught up with the unicorn.

Bert turned away, sad to see such a beautiful creature mutilated. He hurried back up the path that had led him there, wanting to put some distance between himself and the dead unicorn. Seeing the animal made him admit to himself that Jules had been telling the truth. The unicorn had been real, which meant that Bert really was back in the past, with no way to get home. He tried repeating, "I'm not scared of nothing, me," but the words stuck in his throat.

"Jules can't save her unicorn now," he thought, as he carried on walking. "It's too late. She'd better worry about saving me instead. She's got to get me back to me own time. I mean, what am I supposed to do here? Even if I had me brush with me I couldn't get no work as a crossing sweeper. There ain't no proper roads to sweep."

Bert stopped walking. He thought he could hear someone up ahead of him. It sounded like a girl's voice, singing softly, though he was too far away to make out the words. He ran up the path calling out, "Jules? Jules, is that you?" He rounded a bend in the track and found himself face to face with the young woman Jules had seen earlier trying to call the unicorn. She was still carrying the metal flask and the small bundle she'd had with her earlier in the day.

Bert halted abruptly and stared at the woman in surprise. He was disappointed that he hadn't found Jules after all. The young woman put her finger to her lips and said, "Shsh, boy. Don't make so much noise or you'll frighten it away."

"Frighten what away?" said Bert, confused.

"The unicorn. I'm trying to call it, get it to come to me. They're supposed to come out of hiding if a girl sings to them."

"Oh no," thought Bert. "Not another girl trying to find the unicorn." He cleared his throat and said awkwardly, "I'm afraid it ain't going to come to you, whether you sing or not. It's dead. I just found its body further down the path. Someone's gone and killed it and chopped off its horn."

"Then we've lost everything," said the girl, dismayed.

"I don't know why you're getting so upset. Seems to me it's the unicorn that's got the right to feel a bit hard done by, not you. Especially as it was the very last one."

Seeing that she was starting to cry Bert, who was a kind boy, passed her his handkerchief, already damp from Jules using it earlier. The girl pulled herself together and stopped crying. She wiped her eyes with the hanky and handed it back to Bert.

"I'm sorry," the girl replied embarrassed, "but the unicorn was our only chance."

"Only chance for what?" asked Bert.

"To save our farm… "

"Your farm?" said Bert. "What were you planning to do, stick a harness on it and use it as a plough horse?"

"No," said the girl, "it was the horn I needed."

"You were going to chop its horn off?" Bert was horrified.

"No," she replied quickly. "I'd never do that." She held out the metal flask. "I was going to ask it to dip its horn into this flask of water. Unicorns' horns are magical. They make sick people better and if even a little of its magic dissolved into the water, it would have been enough to help my father. He's old and weak, you see. He can't work the land any more. I hoped the unicorn's magic would make him strong again, but now it's too late. The unicorn's dead and we'll lose our farm."

"Can't you find some other way to save the farm?" asked Bert. "You could pay someone to help you with the work."

"We couldn't pay enough," she answered. "We could give someone a place to live and a share of our food, but not much more. No-one would be willing to work for so little."

"I've worked for less," muttered Bert.

"I don't suppose you're looking for work?" she asked, hopefully.

"Not here I'm not. I don't belong here."

"I shouldn't have asked you," said the girl, apologetically. "Farming's hard work when you're not used to it."

"Oh, I can do the work, miss… "

"Rowan, my name's Rowan."

"It's not that, Rowan, it's just that I'm on my way somewhere."

"Of course," said Rowan, trying to hide her disappointment. "Have you had a long journey? Where have you come from?"

"Don't ask," said Bert quickly. "I mean, you wouldn't believe the answer."

"You must be very hungry. I have a little food with me if you'd like to share it, boy."

"Thanks, and the name's Bert."

Rowan opened her small bundle of food and shared the chunk of bread that she had brought with her. Bert munched on his portion gratefully. It had been a long time since his last meal.

As they ate Rowan told him about her father's farm and what they had managed to grow there before her father grew old. It made Bert feel homesick for the time he'd spent working on the land with his granddad.

"You're welcome to sleep in our barn tonight, if you need a place to stay before you continue your journey," she offered. "We've room enough."

"Thanks, but there's someone I need to find," he answered, "then I'm hoping to be on me way home."

"What's your home like?" asked Rowan.

Bert didn't like to admit that he had no home. That he lived on the streets of a city that was probably bigger and richer than anywhere Rowan had ever seen, but that he didn't even have a bed to call his own. If he was lucky and earned some money, he could buy the use of a mattress in the corner of a crowded cellar for a few hours' sleep. If he didn't earn enough for that, he slept in shop doorways trying to keep out of the wind and rain.

"It's alright," he lied, in answer to her question, adding more truthfully. "It's where I belong, anyway."

"If you change your mind, I meant what I said about work," said Rowan, as she wrapped up the flask in her bundle and stood up. "We'd share what we've got with you and pay you what we could."

"It's a kind offer, miss, and I wish I could take you up on it. It's the first chance I've had for proper work, and a place to stay, but it's come at the wrong time... I mean, in the wrong time. Several hundred years too early, I reckon." Rowan looked at him questioningly. "Never mind, miss, I can't explain." He looked round at the forest wistfully. It didn't seem so bad now he wasn't alone in it. "Shame," he said, "I like the countryside better than a town any day. Still, I don't belong here and that's that."

Rowan turned and started to walk back the way she'd come.

"Rowan, I'm sorry about the unicorn," said Bert, as she left.

"So am I," Rowan called back, "but at least I can stop searching for it now. I'll go home and help my father and do what I can on the farm. I wish you well for your journey, Bert."

"Thanks."

He watched her walk away up the path into the distance. She'd just turned off on to a side track when Jules came running down the path towards him.

"Bert, there you are," she called as she slowed down. "I've been looking for you everywhere."

"I should hope so," said Bert indignantly, "since you're the one as got me stuck here."

"I've been looking for the unicorn too," she added, "but I can't find it."

Bert said as gently as he could "I'm sorry Jules, but it's dead. I found its body earlier. You're too late to save it."

"Dead?" Jules' face began to crumple up. "Then the whole thing's been a complete waste of time," she sobbed. "I've searched all through history and come up with loads of ideas and it hasn't made any difference at all. The unicorn's dead and I didn't even get to see it again."

Bert rummaged in his pocket and produced the grimy old handkerchief that now looked as though it had been used once too often. He sighed, "I know it's bad and I'm sorry that it's gone but now, since we can't do nothing to save the unicorn, perhaps you'd better get us both back where we belong."

"I can't," said Jules guiltily. In spite of the state of the handkerchief, she blew her nose loudly into it. "I can only get one of us back. It's a bit complicated, but we've ended up with only one trip through time left and it's yours."

"Mine?"

"Yes," said Jules, trying to sound brave. "You can go home."

"What about you?" asked Bert.

Jules shook her head. "If you didn't want to use your journey, you could give it to me. Otherwise, I'm stuck here."

"And if I give you my turn, I'm stuck here," objected Bert. "It's not fair. Why should I have to make a decision? Everyone wants me to do something for them. Rowan wants me to help on the farm, you want my turn with that time machine. Why should I help either of you? All I want is to go home."

"Me too," said Jules sadly.

"What's your home like?" Bert asked her suddenly. "Got any family?"

Jules nodded. "Mum, dad, and a sister. They're alright. We argue a bit sometimes but I miss them, I want to go back."

"I don't have any family," said Bert slowly. "Nor a proper home, but it's still where I belong. I understand life there. I fit in. Here, it would be like starting all over again."

"I understand," said Jules, and she did. All the time she'd been searching for Bert in the forest she'd been imagining what it would be like to be stuck in the past forever. The idea terrified her; there was no reason Bert should find it any easier.

Bert took the time machine and was about to open the lid when he stopped and looked at Jules. "It's no good. I can't just leave you here. You've got a life to go back to and a family. What have I got? Nothing! Maybe I should stay and help Rowan. I might be able to make a life for myself here."

"Who's Rowan?" asked Jules cautiously. She desperately wanted to go home, but she couldn't just abandon Bert. After all, it was her fault he was stuck here.

"She's a lady I met earlier while I was searching for you. She's offered me a job on her farm."

"Is that what you want to do?"

"Why not?" answered Bert. "I've always liked working in the country and I'll have a roof over me head. Better than sleeping in shop doorways, anyhow."

"Are you sure?" asked Jules.

"Yes," said Bert firmly. He handed Jules the box. "You take it and good luck to you. I hope it gets you home safely. Now, I'd better be off. I have to catch up with Rowan before she gets too far."

"Thank you, Bert," said Jules, trying hard not to cry.

"That's alright, Jules, but just you remember this when you get home. Whatever you set your mind to, you got to keep on trying. Giving up never solves anything."

Bert set off up the track. Jules watched him turn off down the side path Rowan had taken.

"Good luck, Bert," she called, but he was too far away to hear her. In a few minutes he was out of sight and Jules was alone in the forest. She lifted the lid of the box and the mist rose out of it for the last time.

Discussion points

1. Why did Bert decide to stay in the past?

2. Rowan thought the unicorn's horn could heal her father. Are there any animals hunted today because people think parts of their bodies have magical powers or special properties? (See under 'Hunting' in the background notes at the start of the book.)

Activity

Ask the children if they've been to a zoo? If so, which one? What do they think of zoos? Some children may object on principle and should have the chance to say why. If anyone objects to zoos point out that the next game may get them to rethink how they feel about them.

Into the Cage Game

One way of saving animals is to take them out of their threatened environment and place them in a zoo. This protects them from hunters and can maintain a population while efforts are made to restore or protect their habitats. For some species, zoos are their only safe refuge and many zoos do very valuable conservation work. However, providing for the needs of animals in zoos often involves a compromise between the requirements of the animals and of their human visitors.

Explain this to the pupils, then get them to stand in a big circle. This circle represents the boundary of the cage. Take a volunteer out of the circle to be the animal in the cage. We generally suggest that they should be a monkey (you can pick a different animal but do try and choose one that needs trees to climb or perch on).

Now ask the group about what the animal needs and move other volunteers from the circle into the cage to be those objects/animals/features.

For example, if someone suggests the monkey needs company you need to add in another volunteer to be an additional monkey.

After a few minutes the cage should be filled with the following:

> Two 'monkeys'
> Several 'trees' for climbing
> A water trough
> Food bowls
> Some kind of den to hide in.

Get your volunteers to take up the shapes of the objects they represent, for example trees need to stand up with their arms out and fingers spread.

Now go round the pupils who are still forming the circle and ask if they can all see the monkeys. At least some of them won't be able to because trees, dens etc.. will block their view.

Ask the group why they go to a zoo? The usual answer is to see the animals. Ask if they'd make a second visit to a zoo if they hardly saw any animals on their first visit? Most people wouldn't bother.

Let the group go back into a circle (it's tiring standing as a tree for too long).

Remind the pupils that zoos rely on people paying to come to the zoo in order to have the money to feed and care for the animals. This means exhibits have to be designed to allow visitors to see the animals, even if the animals prefer not to be seen or would choose to have a much more densely packed cage, e.g. the monkeys might choose to have far more trees, but then no-one would be able to see them properly.

However, if the long-term plan is to put animals back into the wild, they need to be kept in as natural a habitat as possible.

Re-introduction to the wild can also be quite difficult. Even little differences between wild and captive conditions can cause big problems.

Branches

(To demonstrate this example you will need a strong plastic or wooden ruler or a real branch.)

When a group of monkeys were returned to the wild after growing up in captivity, they all ran up the trees in their release site and then fell off the branches as they tried to run along them. Tell the pupils this story and ask if anyone can guess why.

The answer is that in the zoo where they had grown up, the branches in their cages were fixed to the walls at both ends. Get two volunteers to come up and hold the ruler firmly between them, one holding each end. Now tap the ruler along its length. The ruler will stay fairly rigid.

Of course, in the wild branches are only fixed at one end. To demonstrate the difference tell one of your volunteers to let go of their end of the ruler, while the other keeps their end in its original position. Now tap along the length of the ruler and there should be a visible difference. The pupils should be able to see that there is far more movement at the unfixed end of the ruler or branch. In other words, a real branch is springy when you run along it, while a branch fixed at both ends is not.

The monkeys had to be brought back into captivity, given the chance to learn how to balance on springy branches and then released into the wild again.

The Last Unicorn : Lesson 5 Worksheet

Building a Zoo

In the story, Jules tried to design a zoo but she didn't really know what the animals needed.

If you had to design and run a zoo, what do you think you would need?

For the animals	For human visitors

Which animals would you most like to save?

_____

_____

_____

_____

Pick one of the animals you've listed above and try to find out more about it from the internet or wildlife documentaries. What would this particular animal need if you were to try to keep it in a zoo?

Food

Drink

Habitat

Special features

Some of you will have found that your chosen animal had very distinctive and specific needs. In a zoo every single species has its own specific requirements and providing all of these, along with facilities for human visitors, is a complicated business.

Lesson 6

Jules learns that sad endings can also be happy beginnings

Recap

Question: What had happened to the unicorn?

Answer: It had been killed.

Question: How did Jules get back to the distant past?

Answer: Wiz gave her one of Bert's time journeys.

Question: What happened to Bert?

Answer: He found work on Rowan's farm.

Miss Denton was pacing up and down in the school hall. Her feet, in their shiny blue shoes, were beginning to hurt. She'd been pacing for most of the afternoon when she should have been doing paperwork in her office. Wiz had promised to have Jules back in school by three o'clock at the latest and it was five to three now.

Not that she didn't trust Wiz, of course. She'd known him for years, ever since he'd moved into the house next door. She had been a little surprised when she'd discovered her new next door neighbour was a wizard, but she'd got used to him eventually.

Now she looked after his house whenever he was away somewhere or somewhen. Fed his cat and his bat and his snake and his rat, and all the other creatures that assembled on his doorstep expecting dinner. She found it reassuring that the animals liked him. They were usually good judges of character.

He normally brought her something back from his travels, as a thank you present. Sometimes it was a nice ornament she could put on her mantelpiece, sometimes it was something she didn't feel she could display. Like the time he went to Egypt and brought her back a photograph of the pyramids being built! That kind of thing tended to make people ask awkward questions.

Now she was beginning to regret asking Wiz to try and teach Juliette Baylis something. What if the child never came back? What if she was lost in time forever? How was Miss Denton supposed to explain that? After all, she was responsible for Juliette's welfare. She wasn't trying to punish the girl, just show her how important it was to be willing to learn things.

Miss Denton genuinely liked Juliette and was sure that the child was really intelligent, if only she'd apply herself. It was the fact that the girl didn't want to listen and didn't see the point of learning, that drove Miss Denton to distraction.

That's why, eventually, she'd asked Wiz to help. Now she wished she hadn't. She thought about phoning the police, to report Juliette as a missing person, but how could she possibly explain it to them? She looked at her watch for the thousandth time. It was exactly three o'clock.

Jules suddenly materialised in the school hall, still clutching the carved wooden box. Miss Denton felt faint with relief. Jules sank down on to the floor and began to shake. It was shock, of course, mixed with sheer gratitude at finally getting back to her own time. There had been moments when Jules had really felt she'd never get home. Not that the school was home exactly, but Jules was more pleased to see it than she'd ever expected to be in her life.

Miss Denton hurried over to her saying, "Juliette? Are you alright? I've been so worried about you."

Jules looked up at the teacher in surprise. Miss Denton? Worried? She'd thought the deputy head hated her.

Suddenly Wiz appeared beside them making them both jump. "I hate it when you do that," said Jules and Miss Denton in unison.

Wiz just smiled at them, then reached down and helped Jules to her feet.

"I see Bert let you have his last time journey," he said to Jules, taking the box from her.

"Yes," she replied, "wasn't that kind of him? I was so afraid I'd be stuck there forever."

"Whilst instead, Bert's stuck there forever," said the Wiz dryly.

"Yes," said Jules sadly, "though I think he might manage to make a life for himself there. Wiz?" She looked up at him pleadingly. "Will you go and see him sometimes, and make sure he's alright?"

Wiz thought for a moment and answered casually, "I suppose I might drop in, if I'm passing."

"Please?" begged Jules.

"Oh alright," grinned Wiz. "I was only teasing you. Of course I'll keep an eye on him. After all, we're all responsible for him being there."

Miss Denton looked ashamed, even though she didn't know exactly what she was supposed to be being ashamed of.

"I'm sorry about all this, Juliette," she said, apologetically. "I don't know what went on today, but it was my idea to have Wiz try and teach you something."

Jules was amazed. A teacher? Apologising to her?

"That's alright, Miss Denton, and I did learn something, I think."

"What?" asked Miss Denton.

"That I don't know enough to do anything right," Jules said gloomily.

"I'm sure that is not true, dear," Miss Denton tried to sound encouraging. Jules didn't look at all encouraged.

"I think it's time you put the kettle on, Miss Denton. I'm sure we could all do with some tea."

Miss Denton took the hint and left Jules alone with Wiz. Wiz led Jules over to a bench and sat her down.

"Don't be so hard on yourself, Jules," he said, sitting beside her. "You have learnt a lot today."

"Bert said I had to keep on trying, but what's the point? I didn't save the unicorn. It's dead. I didn't know enough to help it."

"Realising there are things you don't know is the first step towards learning anything. You may not have saved the unicorn, but there are other creatures that need saving."

"Like what?" Jules asked curiously.

"Things from your own time, from your own country even. All sorts of animals need help. Even ordinary creatures like sparrows are getting rarer all the time."

"Sparrows?" exclaimed Jules. She was about to laugh at the idea when she remembered her visit to the future. Now she thought about it, she hadn't seen or heard any birds at all there.

"So what's the point in trying to save things?" she retorted angrily. "I've been to the future and there are hardly any animals left, so how can anything I do make a difference?"

"You haven't seen the future, Jules, just one possible version of it. You can't change the past (that's why you couldn't save the unicorn, but you can work in the present to change the future. You can help to save the animals we have got left, so that we don't lose any more."

"You mean the future could be different?"

"Yes," said Wiz smiling. "Look."

The patterns flowing across his gown formed into a series of pictures. In some the earth looked withered and empty, like the version of the future Jules had seen, but others showed different possibilities. A world where people and animals could exist together, another where trees were being planted rather than felled. In one image the rivers and seas had been cleaned up and the oceans were full of fish and whales. There were so many possibilities.

"But what can I do?" asked Jules.

"You can tell people what you've learned," said Wiz. "You passed the test I set you. You realised that you needed to learn more and that the past has things to teach you. That it's worth trying to save what you can. All you have to do is communicate that to other people."

"But what if they won't listen to me?"

"Most people will, if you can convince them how important it is. A lot of people are willing to learn."

"Unless they already know everything, like you," said Jules, teasingly.

"I told you before," said Wiz, "I don't know everything." More seriously he added, "I make mistakes too. I almost got you killed today when I sent you into the future. I'm sorry, Jules."

"It's alright. You're the one who rescued me," said Jules. "But if you don't have all the answers either, how are we supposed to know what to do? How can we change the future?"

"We'll just have to work it out together," said Wiz. "Everyone will." Wiz stood up. "Come on, that kettle should be boiled by now."

Jules stood up to join him saying, "I can't believe how far I've travelled today."

"Far?" The wizard burst out laughing. "You've gone no distance at all. You haven't been further than a few hundreds metres from this spot all day. It's time you've been travelling through, not space."

"You mean all those places were on this very spot?"

"Exactly. You never left the school grounds."

"Are you saying that the unicorn was once right here?" asked Jules, incredulously.

"Yes," answered Wiz, "but hundreds of years ago."

They walked into the staff room where Miss Denton was waiting for them with mugs of tea.

"Here you are, Juliette." The teacher handed her one of the steaming mugs. "You've just got time to drink it before the bell goes."

Jules drank thirstily, thinking about how glad she'd be to see her family again. She spilt some tea as she put the mug down on the table. Reaching forward to mop it up she realised she still had Bert's soggy, grubby hanky in her hand. She put it carefully in her pocket to remind her of everything that had happened that day. The school bell rang and she got up to leave.

"Well, goodbye, Wiz. Thanks for everything."

"Goodbye, Jules," said Wiz, then noticing she seemed a little sad he added, "You are alright, aren't you?"

"Yes, I'm fine. I just wish I could have seen the unicorn one last time, that's all."

"Perhaps you will," said Wiz, smiling at her. "Look up at the sky one night. There's a legend that says when the last unicorn died it became a cluster of stars, watching over the earth. If you look carefully you may be able to see it."

"Really?" asked Jules excitedly. "Is it true?"

"Who knows," laughed Wiz, "but it's a brilliant story, isn't it?"

"And even a story can teach you something," chimed in Miss Denton. "As long as you're willing to learn."

Discussion points

1. Did Jules' adventures help her to change her mind about things?

If so, what?

2. Wiz said that it's impossible to change the past, but what did he say we could do?

"Today is where we start to build the future."

Activity

Get the children to pair up and play scissors, paper, stone. In case anyone is unfamiliar with the game, here is a brief description:

Each child has to decide which hand shape to produce out of the following:

Scissors (hand held sideways with first and middle fingers pointing forwards

and slightly apart, and the other two fingers and the thumb curled into the palm.

Paper (hand held flat, palm downwards.)

Stone (hand clenched into a fist.)

On the count of three each child must take up one of those positions.

Within the pairs, if both pick the same shape it's a draw.

If one picks scissors and one paper – scissors win (scissors cut paper).

If one picks scissors and the other stone – stone wins (stone breaks scissors).

If one picks stone and the other picks paper – paper wins (paper can wrap stones).

As the final chapter is shorter than the others, there are two games in this section. If you only have time for one, use 'Threes' but if at all possible include the 'Hope' game as well.

Threes Game

This game is about bringing together some of the ideas that the earlier games have explored. Remind the pupils that so far you've looked at three different ways to try and save animal species:

▶ Taking the *animal* and putting it in a zoo.

▶ Protecting the *place* where the animal lives.

▶ Educating *people* to care for the animals.

Ask the pupils to get into groups of three, then explain that they're going to be playing a game similar to scissors, paper, stone.

Set up three hand signals:

For saving *animals* we used two forefingers sticking up above the head like horns.

For saving *places* we used both hands held out flat.

For educating *people* we used one hand held across the body, the palm against the heart.

On a count of three, they must all take up one of those three positions, indicating which they think is a good way of saving animal species. (Don't give them time to confer with their group.)

The only groups that would have achieved their goal of saving endangered species and maintaining the balance of nature are the ones where one of each sign had been used (e.g. animal/place/people all in the same group of three).

Give them another go at the game. Without conferring, the chances of success are low, as the choices are random.

Ask the pupils how they could increase the chances of getting all three in their group. They will realise they would have to consult with each other and agree who was going to do what.

Give them a chance to do that, then repeat the game. Now each group should have one of each sign in it (animal/place/people).

Explain that this process of conferring and planning is an important part of modern conservation. All three aspects of conservation are needed, but are usually tackled by very different groups and organisations. These different organisations must consult each other and work together to co-ordinate their efforts, if their long-term conservation aims are to be achieved.

The Hope Game

For this game you will need four paper or cardboard signs. Write the word 'Common' on one, 'Recovering' on the next, 'Endangered' on the third and 'Extinct' on the last one.

This game is to encourage your pupils about conservation and help them to see that the news isn't all bad.

First, show your group the cards and ask them what those words mean in the context of animal species. (Recovering is where a species has been on the verge of extinction but numbers are now rising.)

Fix the signs up in different places in the room. Explain that you are going to call out the names of different animals and the pupils have to move towards the sign that they think best describes the population status of that animal.

Start by calling out a couple of easy ones to start with:

Dinosaur (extinct)

Rabbit   (common)

Now call out animals off the following list. If the pupils don't know a particular animal, encourage them to take a guess and pick a sign to move towards.

In some cases the group will be split. This is particularly true of 'Recovering' animals where some will go to 'Endangered' and others to 'Recovering.' In this case explain that they are both right to some extent because the recovering animals have been endangered before efforts were made to protect them.

Tigers	(endangered)
Dodos	(extinct)
Pink pigeon	(recovering)
Zebra	(common)
Otters	(recovering)
Giant panda	(endangered)
Great auk	(extinct)
Koala	(recovering)
Mountain gorilla	(endangered)
Woolly mammoth	(extinct)
Bald eagle	(recovering)
Magpie	(common)
American alligator	(recovering)
Rodrigues fruit bat	(recovering)

The fact that so many species are recovering shows that there is hope. People can make a difference, if they work together to try to help an endangered species.

A good example of this is the Rodrigues fruit bat. In the 1970s the numbers of this bat had dropped to less than 100 animals. They live on a tiny island in the Indian Ocean and are the only native mammals there so are an important part of the island's ecosystem.

The numbers had fallen for three reasons:

1.   The island is in the cyclone belt and when a tropical storm hits many bats get killed and much of their habitat is destroyed.

2.   Humans moving on to the island were clearing the trees to move on to the land or for firewood.

3.   Humans were hunting them for sport.

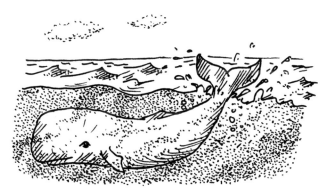

In the 1970s Gerald Durrell, the Founder of Jersey Zoo (now the Durrell Wildlife Conservation Trust) got permission to collect 10-12 of the remaining bats on the island and started to breed them in his zoo in Jersey, splitting them with other zoos when the size of the colony increased.

Also, a local captive breeding and release programme was started. Certain areas of the island are being reforested (trees are being planted for the future).

An education programme was set up to teach the local people about their bats and how important they are to the island (they are one of the main dispersers of seeds) and explain why they shouldn't be hunted (hunting was also made illegal).

Due to these measures the population on the island has now increased to about 1600-2000 (in 2001) while the captive population in zoos around the world now stands at about 500/600 (in 2001). These bats are kept as a standby population, which could be released back on to the island if another cyclone were to destroy a large proportion of the wild bat population.

The Last Unicorn: Lesson 6 Worksheet

Co-operation

Fill in the name of the animal you would most like to save from extinction below:

_____

(It can be the same animal you used in the Building a Zoo worksheet but try to think of a different one.)

Fill in the name of the type of habitat or environment you would most like to save for the future:

_____

(This can be anything from a meadow to a coral reef.)

Fill in a human attitude towards animals or the environment that you would most like to change:

_____

_____

Now look at your three choices. If you've chosen whales, the ocean and water pollution as your three issues, it would be fairly easy to develop a plan where all three aspects of the project are working towards the same end.

Not so easy if you've chosen tigers, your garden and hunting.

Tigers and hunting may be correct, but protecting your garden can't help tigers (though it will help a lot of local wildlife).

Imagine your three choices have actually been picked by three different conservation organisations. You're all trying to help conserve wildlife in your own way and are totally committed to the animal/habitat or educational method you've chosen.

You know that if you all work together you can be more effective, but that might mean you have to be prepared to change the focus of your work, for example, swap from trying to save gardens to trying to save forests.

Would you find this difficult? If so, why?

Would you try to negotiate, for example, "I'll help you with your project if you'll help me with what I want to do later"? Do you think this would work, and why might it succeed or fail?

Sometimes the urgency of a situation is more important than our likes and dislikes. For certain animals there is very little time left, but don't give up hope. We can make a difference if we try.

Don't forget to visit our website for all our latest publications, news and reviews.

www.luckyduck.co.uk

New publications every year on our specialist topics:

▸ **Emotional Literacy**

▸ **Self-esteem**

▸ **Bullying**

▸ **Positive Behaviour Management**

▸ **Circle Time**

▸ **Anger Management**

▸ **Asperger's Syndrome**

▸ **Eating Disorders**

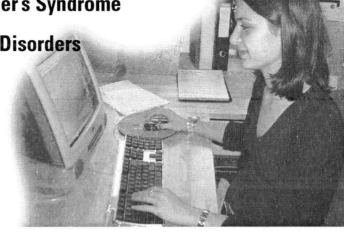

3 Thorndale Mews, Clifton, Bristol, BS8 2HX | Tel: +44 (0) 117 973 2881 Fax: +44 (0) 117 973 1707